S0-CFE-147

Cultivating Your Creative Life

Exercises, Activities & Inspiration for
Finding Balance, Beauty & Success as an Artist

Cultivating Your Creative Life

Exercises, Activities & Inspiration for
Finding Balance, Beauty & Success as an Artist

Alena Hennessy

Quarry Books
100 Cummings Center, Suite 406L
Beverly, MA 01915

quarrybooks.com • craftside.typepad.com

© 2012 by Quarry Books
Text © 2012 Alena Hennessy

First published in the United States of America in 2012 by
Quarry Books, a member of
Quayside Publishing Group
100 Cummings Center
Suite 406-L
Beverly, Massachusetts 01915-6101
Telephone: (978) 282-9590
Fax: (978) 283-2742
www.quarrybooks.com
Visit www.Craftside.Typepad.com for a behind-the-scenes peek at our crafty world!

All rights reserved. No part of this book may be reproduced in any form without written permission of the copyright owners. All images in this book have been reproduced with the knowledge and prior consent of the artists concerned, and no responsibility is accepted by the producer, publisher, or printer for any infringement of copyright or otherwise, arising from the contents of this publication. Every effort has been made to ensure that credits accurately comply with information supplied. We apologize for any inaccuracies that may have occurred and will resolve inaccurate or missing information in a subsequent reprinting of the book.

10 9 8 7 6 5 4 3 2 1

ISBN: 978-1-59253-786-0

Digital edition published in 2012
eISBN: 978-1-61058-418-0

Library of Congress Cataloging-in-Publication Data

Hennessy, Alena, 1977-
 Cultivating your creative life : exercises, activities, and inspiration for finding balance and success as an artist / Alena Hennessy.
    pages cm
 Summary: "Cultivating Your Creative Life: Exercises, Activities, and Inspiration for Finding Balance, Beauty, and Success as an Artist is a multi-faceted book where creativity and wonder intermingle to show how to live a creative and balanced life while moving toward your goals. You'll delve right into the creative process and find practical and inspiring suggestions on making a living as a working artist. This book holds reverence and respect for the natural world in high esteem, using a central visual metaphor of the growth and blossoming of a tree. Alena Hennessy's illustration style combines nature, whimsey, delicacy, and a modern sensibility; vibrant pen and ink illustrations accompany relevant quotes of inspiration, tips, and creative journal exercises. Cultivating Your Creative Life is not only an interactive creativity guide; it is a work of art, in itself--a beautiful, collectible volume--to save and to savor, or to give as a gift to the special creative person in your life"-- Provided by publisher.
 ISBN 978-1-59253-786-0 (pbk.)
 1. Artists--Psychology. 2. Creation (Literary, artistic, etc.) 3. Self-actualization (Psychology) I. Title.
 N71.H38 2012
 701'.15--dc23
                                                                                    2011050667

Design: Rita Sowins / Sowins Design

All images and artwork by the author with the exception of yoga photography on pages 84, 89, 91, and 93, by Ruslan Tumash.

Printed in China

This book is for you and your
creative life.

Contents

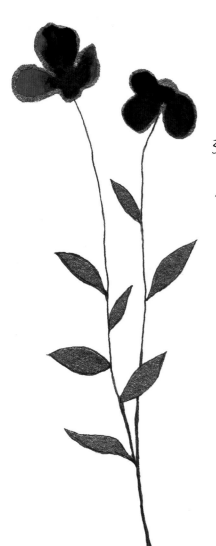

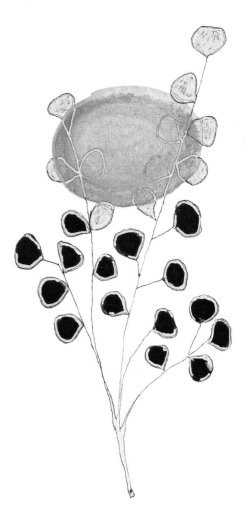

Introduction

We are all born to create. When we are small, everything seems like a creative adventure. Colors inspire, music moves us, and sensations fill our playful beings. The innate artist within us loves to come out and express its unique truth.

As we grow and navigate throughout life, however, we find others will sometimes judge or dissuade, placing doubt into our mind and spirit. Unleashing the creative back to its origins takes some boldness, some surrender, and a little faith.

And yet, it's all so accessible and present. We need to begin to make space and plant seeds so that a beautiful tree can grow. This tree needs to receive nourishment so that it can slowly branch out under the sun and blossom.

Once our creativity has taken root, we need to find ways to support it and help it continue to grow and flourish. This can happen in small steps so that we are gradually moving toward a way of life that feels in harmony with our true selves.

The intent of this book is to give you some building blocks so that you can, over time, move from dreaming about making art or just making art from time to time, to making more art, and then to making a living as a working artist.

As we nurture our creative spirit, we should also pay attention to our physical well-being. When our bodies are in a place of balance and harmony, when our roots are deep and spreading out wide, our creative work can flourish. Herbal remedies, flower essences, a balanced diet, and taking time for fresh air help us as we move forward with intent. Yoga and meditation can keep our minds clear and bodies feeling strong and at ease.

Interacting with a community of artists brings the support we need to stay inspired and allows us to share knowledge and resources. Setting intentions for what we truly want to create in life helps us become better artists and, ultimately, happier with ourselves. The gift of living an authentic life in glowing health and wholeness is a blessing to always strive for.

In this book, you will find many spaces in which to write and draw. You can also work hand in hand with a sketchbook or journal. Assemble a pen and pencil, an eraser, paint, brushes, and whatever other media you like to use to create. Some materials I have used are Golden liquid acrylics, India ink, watercolors, gel pens, decorative collage papers, found plant material, fine art pens, my digital camera, and so forth. I paint on wood panels and thick watercolor paper, but ultimately you will want to follow your instinct on how you would like to create.

While you complete the exercises, remember that you are tending to your own unique muse and child artist within. Experimentation will help you open up and discover what you love. It's crucial not to judge your work or your process along the way.

As you become more creatively in tune, feelings may come up that will need tending to. All of this is good. There are no mistakes along this path, only lessons and deepening into understanding that all of this is a gift.

CHAPTER 1

Planting Seeds

Yesterday my brother and I took a long walk in an old Florida park. I had not planned to spend an afternoon outside. I was visiting over the holidays with my family and we were simply headed out to get some art supplies, stop by the bank, and come back home. At first I hesitated when he suggested the walk, thinking, "There's not enough time." But after the errands were done, I felt myself let go of something and agreed.

We drove under a thick canopy of trees and quietly got out of the car. Not many words were exchanged as we headed toward the rotting boardwalk. As I wandered, I slowly felt my internal state unwinding, my senses heightening and expanding, my world growing bigger with each step.

[SPENDING TIME OUT IN NATURE CAN REFUEL THE SENSES AND CREATIVE RESERVES.]

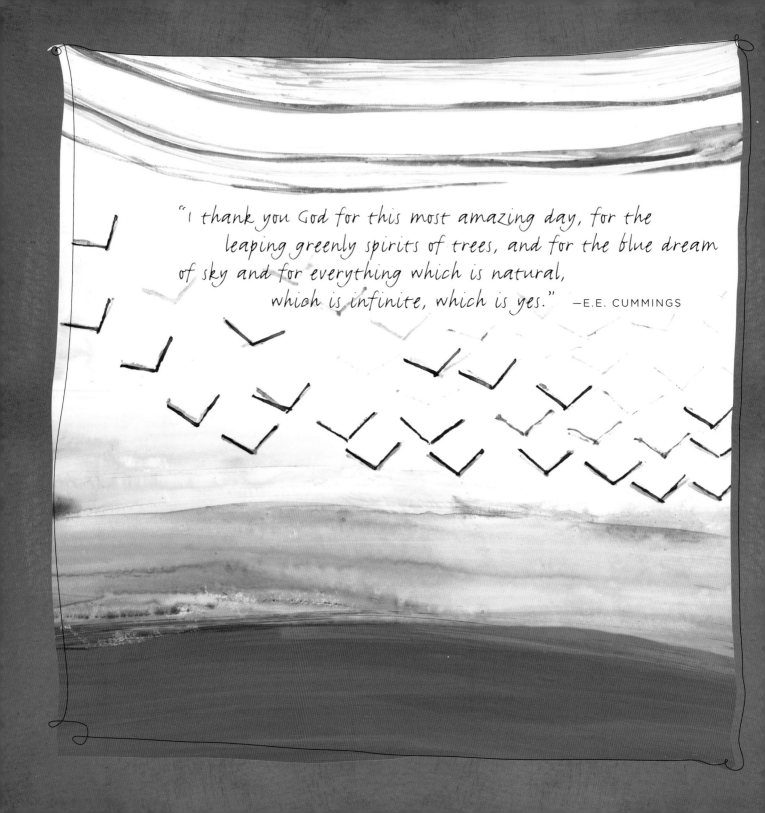

"I thank you God for this most amazing day, for the
        leaping greenly spirits of trees, and for the blue dream
of sky and for everything which is natural,
        which is infinite, which is yes."   —E.E. CUMMINGS

I began to notice the many surrounding sounds and the magical swampland that awaited us. I heard the gentle cry of the osprey and felt the comfort of the creaking wood beneath my feet. I looked up and saw light was filtering and flickering through old cypress trees, their silver moss hanging down in delicate gentleness.

The water underneath the boardwalk stretched out to the horizon, the ripples of dancing white light and the vast blue hue reflected in the water. I was struck by the thick algae that formed in earthen masses. It held worlds of life in it, as numerous birds hunted and fed on tiny fish and crawlers. I felt my mind and heart expanding into my environment with each passing minute.

We then decided to climb a two-story wooden tower that looked out over this large body of deep blue. I only saw life: living, breathing, and in constant motion. Looking out from the tower, I remembered the Buddhist term *annica*.

Annica means impermanence, or life being in a state of constant change and motion. I saw this. The river danced and moved, carrying things with it. I felt stillness, and yet everything around me was moving. It dawned on me that feeling still when everything is changing around you is vital to understanding life. The cycle of birth and death continues and does not stop for anyone.

As artists we tend to play with motion. We love things that are kinesthetic. A repeated stroke with a pen or paintbrush seems like a natural desire that wants to be expressed.

[REPEATED MARKS OR STROKES FROM A BRUSH CAN
GIVE AN ART PIECE A SENSE OF MOVEMENT.]

As we begin to see the world more vividly around us, the more we can find inspiration from our own work. A simple walk in a park can prove awe-inspiring. The experience is then stored in our creative reserves and brought back with us to the studio. The more our eyes open, ears listen, and skin feels, the more we have to give back to our work. It's almost as if we are creating space within ourselves so that more of our original ideas can grow. In order to do that, however, we need to clear things out, or go through a process of unlearning.

The process of unlearning what we are taught or what others think of us may prove to be just as valuable as the learning itself. This is when we gradually clear out others' judgments and opinions, and start understanding and listening to our own beings. No one thinks like you, talks like you, or makes art like you, and that is an extraordinary thing.

At the beginning of the unlearning process, it can be helpful to make a list of things you have picked up from others that you want to drop. These can be anything, really. For instance, I love to sing and have since I was little. I have often had fantasies about being a singer, of baring my soul to a small audience in a sparkly peasant dress. I imagine what it would be like to have a voice like Björk, Regina Spektor, or even Nina Simone; just the unnerving thrill to be able to perform. But because someone once told me my singing voice wasn't so great, I happen to believe that also, and thus I haven't explored it much. This doesn't mean I won't take singing lessons someday. In fact, I have some plans set with friends for a night of some serious karaoke singing. So, on my list of thoughts I want to drop, I would write "I can't sing."

"Change alone is eternal, perpetual, immortal."

—ARTHUR SCHOPENHAUER

[A SIMPLE COLOR-WASH PAINTING CAN BE A MEDITATIVE EXPERIENCE. THIS CAN BE DONE BY EMPTYING YOUR MIND OF ANY THOUGHTS WHILE YOU PAINT AND ALLOWING YOUR BRUSH TO SPEAK FOR YOU THROUGH COLOR. THIS IMAGE WAS CREATED BY WATERED-DOWN WATERCOLOR AND INK OVER A JOURNAL ENTRY TO CREATE A "FRESH NEW FIELD." DO THIS BY ADDING A GOOD AMOUNT OF WATER TO YOUR BRUSH AND ONTO THICK WATERCOLOR PAPER, THEN DIP YOUR BRUSH INTO THE PAINTS AND BLEND DIRECTLY ON THE PAPER. YOU CAN ALSO ADD DETAILS, INCLUDING WORDS, WITH PENS OR MARKERS. THE GOLD CIRCLES WERE MADE USING A GEL PEN.]

"Write down the thoughts of the moment. Those that come unsought for are commonly the most valuable."

—FRANCIS BACON

[A PEN, INK, AND WATERCOLOR PAINTING EXHIBIT
THE IDEA OF A NEW LANDSCAPE OR GARDEN IN BLOOM
UNDER A FULL BLUE MOON.]

"You are today where your thoughts have
brought you; you will be tomorrow where
your thoughts take you." —JAMES ALLEN

EXERCISE Write and Release

» Write out a list of thoughts to weed out or things you think about yourself that you no longer want to carry. Let this be an instinctual process and do not censure yourself. Don't worry about complete sentences—this can be written in stream-of-consciousness fragments or even with single words.

» After your list is complete, survey it for a little while. It's important to recognize and accept that these thoughts were things you may have carried for years. Notice any patterns you see and take personal note of them. Now you can transform these thoughts into emptiness. They were stuck inside of you. But since they were never yours to begin with, you can let go of them.

» Turn these thoughts into a drawing. For instance, you could draw different-size thought bubbles to represent different items on the list, each marked with an X or other expressive symbol. Or paint over the list with a color wash, or erase it and turn it into a minimalist drawing. You can do anything, really, just as long as it expresses the fact that you don't own these ideas anymore.

» Maybe you would like to make a collage with decorative papers and paints, or include a photograph of yourself as a child in the center. There is no wrong way to transform this journal entry into a work of art; the point is just to transform it. Take the old thoughts and make them beautiful and fresh. This is you anew with an empty field waiting for unsullied seeds to be planted. As your thoughts change about yourself, so will your life.

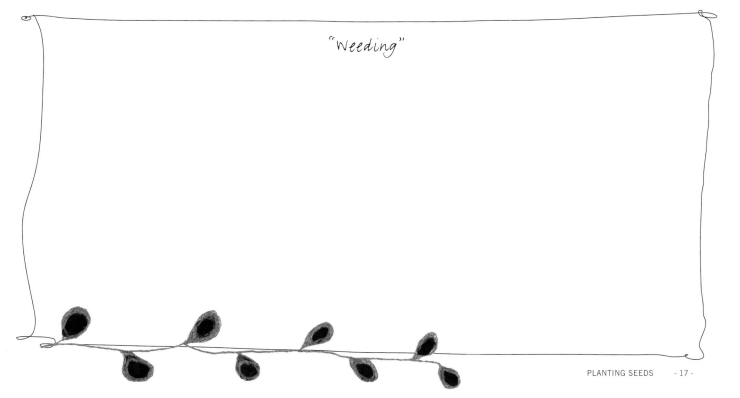

"Weeding"

"Planting New Seeds"

In the space above, make a list of thoughts about yourself that you like. Again, let them flow out of you like water, not thinking too much about what sounds right or what you think would be the correct thing to put down. We are avoiding these notions of right and wrong as much as possible. The thoughts you decide to own are the seeds you are planting for yourself. After you are done, survey these ideas and think about them for a while.

 **EXERCISE** # Draw

Draw and decorate around your words if you like, or leave them alone as a bold list to serve as a frequent reminder.

EXERCISE Contemplate

Write about the following:

» **Think** about someone you truly admire. What qualities do you admire about that person? Write those down. Chances are you are attracted to him or her because the two of you are similar. And if you don't see similarities, perhaps it's because the qualities you share haven't been fully expressed yet. Maybe you haven't given yourself a chance to express them. Things that spark our interest and intrigue us are often things that are already innate within us. We are our desires. All we have to do is simply give ourselves permission to embody these qualities. But this starts first with recognizing what seeds we want to plant in our life.

I admire:

» In what ways can you clear space in your life (be it of people, habits, or things)? The goal is to make room for new possibilities to grow as an artist and a person. Write about things that you know are not helping you attain these goals.

To clear:

_____

_____

_____

_____

» What people, habits, or things can you bring into your life that will help you plant seeds of new growth? You will want to bring in anything that will give you sustenance and new energy.

To grow:

_____

_____

_____

_____

 # EXERCISE Draw

Draw around and decorate your thoughts. On a fresh page, turn your thoughts into a work of art. It can be a simple painting or drawing or an outrageous collage full of varying images. All this is a reflection of your unique nature as a human being and an artist. There is no wrong or right way to do this; it can be anything.

 **EXERCISE** # Document

» **Design** a work of art that represents the life of a seed. What process does a seed go through to become a tree or flower? Imagine what that experience would be like.

» **Research** a seed's growth process online or in books. In your sketchbook, break up a page into three equal rows and columns using a ruler so that the page has at least three but no more than nine boxes. Break down a seed's transformation into a flower in each box so that the first box is a simple seed and the last a flower in full bloom.

"The Life of a seed"

{ A PHOTO SERIES THAT REPRESENTS NEW GROWTH: THE TWO OUTER PHOTOS WERE TAKEN BY LOOKING STRAIGHT UP INTO A TREE USING THE HIPSTAMATIC IPHONE APPLICATION.}

"And the day came when the risk to remain tight in a bud more painful than the risk it took to blossom."

—ANAÏS NIN

"A morning glory at my window satisfies me more than the metaphysics of books."

—WALT WHITMAN

Go Further

Make a drawing, painting, collage, photo series, digital work, or anything that symbolizes a fresh garden to you. It does not even have to look like a garden. Just let it be full of things that represent new growth.

Make a little garden to sit next to you while your work. Purchase or make a planter box that can go in your windowsill. Find some seeds that interest you (whether they be aromatic herbs or flowers) and plant them. Water your garden and watch it grow. Document the growth through photos or sketches.

TRY THIS!

» **Clean out your closet!** This process can feel oh-so-liberating. Get rid of clothes that you hardly ever wear but hold on to for whatever reason. Yes, that old frock from the 1980s with the unflattering fit needs to go. Keep only clothes that make you feel good when you wear them. If you have a hesitation about whether to keep something or not, that probably means it needs to go. Take the bag to a local charity and admire the space you've just created.

» **Organize your studio** (even if that means a table in your bedroom or basement). Take your time with this. Get it to the point so that when you sit down to make art, it is an effortless experience and your mind can relax in an uncluttered space. Throw away dead brushes and dried-up paints. Don't get me wrong—a little mess is sometimes fun, but you want your space to breathe order when you walk in.

TIP OF THE TRADE

Browse the Internet to find artists whose style and approach to business inspires you. Study their websites for insight on how they get their work out there. Where do they exhibit? Do they sell their work wholesale, or to stores? What trade or craft shows do they attend? What blogs or magazines have featured their work? Make notes and craft a step-by-step plan to create your own business plan.

Also check out artists' newsletters and online classes for business tips. Many artists, me included, offer such things as e-courses online. You may also want to visit local artists in your area and talk about what works for them. Stop by during open-studio days, attend artists' receptions at galleries, and make observations. If they're open to hearing it, share your personal story with other artists and talk to them about what you (and they) are striving for. Be a keen listener and observer.

Remember to take things step by step, so you have enough time to develop your inherent, unique creative voice. It's important that you craft your business plan gradually, so you have the time to devote to nurturing your creative growth.

You may want to learn a little in computer design programs (such as Photoshop and Illustrator) to create your logo and name. You can also scan your own letters and designs. (A quality scanner is a key item to purchase.) Fonts should be fairly consistent, as should the overall aesthetic. Don't be afraid to experiment and have fun. It's all part of your creative expression! Then, from there, you can begin to share your work with the outside world.

"Creativity has more to do with the elimination of the inessential than with inventing something new."

—HELMUT JAHN

"A tree is an incomprehensible mystery."
—JIM WOODRING

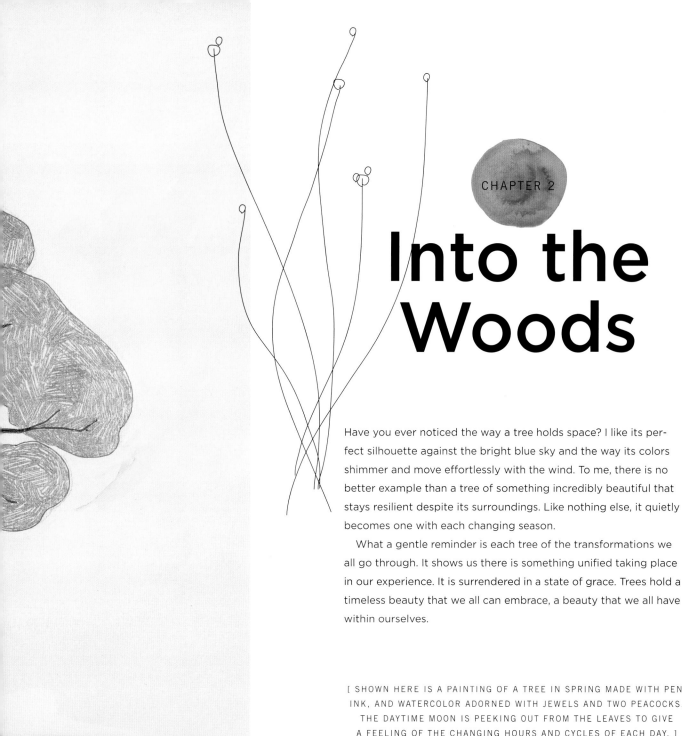

CHAPTER 2

Into the Woods

Have you ever noticed the way a tree holds space? I like its perfect silhouette against the bright blue sky and the way its colors shimmer and move effortlessly with the wind. To me, there is no better example than a tree of something incredibly beautiful that stays resilient despite its surroundings. Like nothing else, it quietly becomes one with each changing season.

What a gentle reminder is each tree of the transformations we all go through. It shows us there is something unified taking place in our experience. It is surrendered in a state of grace. Trees hold a timeless beauty that we all can embrace, a beauty that we all have within ourselves.

[SHOWN HERE IS A PAINTING OF A TREE IN SPRING MADE WITH PEN, INK, AND WATERCOLOR ADORNED WITH JEWELS AND TWO PEACOCKS. THE DAYTIME MOON IS PEEKING OUT FROM THE LEAVES TO GIVE A FEELING OF THE CHANGING HOURS AND CYCLES OF EACH DAY.]

"Keep your love of nature, for that is the true way to understand art more and more."

—VINCENT VAN GOGH

[DRAWING ONLY CERTAIN IMPRESSIONS, IN ABSTRACT
COLORS AND SHAPES, CREATES A MINIMAL BUT
BOLD AND CONTRASTED WORK.]

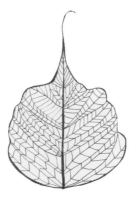

Take your sketchbook with you the next time you walk in the woods. Begin to see the details all around you. Notice how colors intermingle, light reflects, flowers come together in effortless groupings. Observe how numerous shapes can be expressed in one single blossom. Take in how nature seems to dance without any pretentiousness or assumptions, as if it were saying, "The only time is now, and in that, perfection can be found." The beauty of the natural world is so immense and restorative that it can turn any day around.

The next time you are outside, bring a sketchbook, pencil, and eraser. You can also bring pens or any other media that you fancy. Sit beneath a tree and close your eyes. Just allow yourself to follow your breath for five minutes. Notice how your breath moves up and down; allow each exhale to release any tension. When thoughts come, let them pass like clouds, without grasping or trying to control them. Feel every tiny hair on your arms and notice every sound. Hear the birds sing from both near and far away.

Be aware of what feelings or sensations arise in you. Then slowly open your eyes and take it all in. Begin to sketch. Start with exactly where you are, not where you wish you could be. Look out onto the horizon and direct your gaze back to your surroundings. Notice how colors and shapes shift in all directions. You do not need to sketch only what you see, but sketch what you feel as well. Make up shapes and beings. Create a world around you—slowly, without judgment—that expresses what you see in this moment. It can be as literal or imaginary as you want. Begin to ponder: What do I find beautiful? What do I feel when I take in this scenery? Take a little time to draw shapes and observations only. Draw what impresses you. Leave out what is not necessary. Your sketchbook will serve as a visual library with words and images that come directly from you.

*"One must ask children and birds
how cherries and strawberries taste."*

—JOHANN WOLFGANG VON GOETHE

Stress takes away our ability to create, while feeling refreshed opens the doors to our imagination at play. New ideas and ways of thinking can enter our being when we simply change our scenery.

Sometimes, if I am in need of inspiration or ideas, I simply step outside my front door. My little dog and I go on a long walk, up to a favorite city park. The sun begins to hit my skin, and light dances on the neighborhood gardens. It is a simple yet fulfilling experience. I walk noticing the beauty outside of me, instead of the story within me. This way, new narratives, ones that only nature can create, begin to fill me with inspiration. I may notice new shapes I have never seen before, or colors that complement one another that I would not have painted before.

It is from this place that I begin to let go of any expectations I have for myself. I release the doubt-maker inside me and start anew. And as I head back into my studio, I approach each work of art with fresh eyes. I feel more relaxed, and from that place, creativity can flow.

It does not matter whether you are just beginning to discover your own desire to create or you have been making art for years. A nature walk or a trip to the sea can be a time to feel a sense of peace and quietude. The walk can even be around a city block if you take note of every little thing around you. Slow down, and you will notice how everything breathes life and nothing is stagnant. The same is true for you.

Your creative life has begun. It is in motion. Hold it as it opens. Everything that we give attention to will begin to grow. Embrace that notion as you begin to create.

[BOTH MOVEMENT AND STILLNESS ARE EXPRESSED
IN NATURE. A RELAXING TRIP TO THE SEA CAN RENEW THE
SPIRIT AND STIR THE CREATIVE MUSE.]

"In every walk with nature
one receives far more than he seeks." —JOHN MUIR

"Art is the child of Nature; yes, her darling child, in whom we trace the features of the mother's face, her aspect and her attitude." —BECK

[SIMPLE PLEASURES CAN BE FOUND IN TOUCHING AND
TAKING IN NATURAL BEAUTY.]

"Pleasure"

(A Short Poem or Else Not, Say I)
True pleasure breathes not city air,
Nor in Art's temples dwells,
In palaces and towers where
The voice of Grandeur dwells.

No! Seek it where high Nature holds
Her court 'mid stately groves,
Where she her majesty unfolds,
And in fresh beauty moves;

Where thousand birds of sweetest song,
The wildly rushing storm
And hundred streams which glide along,
Her mighty concert form!

Go where the woods in beauty sleep
Bathed in pale Luna's light,
Or where among their branches sweep
The hollow sounds of night.

Go where the warbling nightingale
In gushes rich doth sing,
Till all the lonely, quiet vale
With melody doth ring.

Go, sit upon a mountain steep,
And view the prospect round;
The hills and vales, the valley's sweep,
The far horizon bound.

Then view the wide sky overhead,
The still, deep vault of blue,
The sun which golden light doth shed,
The clouds of pearly hue.

And as you gaze on this vast scene
Your thoughts will journey far,
Though hundred years should roll between
On Time's swift-passing car.

To ages when the earth was young,
When patriarchs, grey and old,
The praises of their god oft sung,
And oft his mercies told.

You see them with their beards of snow,
Their robes of ample form,
Their lives whose peaceful, gentle flow,
Felt seldom passion's storm.

Then a calm, solemn pleasure steals
Into your inmost mind;
A quiet aura your spirit feels,
A softened stillness kind.

—CHARLOTTE BRONTË

moon flower
star shine

EXERCISE Reflect

Answer the following questions in your sketchbook:

» What is one of your earliest childhood memories about nature—something that really stood out as a special experience?

_____

_____

_____

_____

_____

_____

_____

_____

» What are you drawn to when you look outside? What are your favorite animals, plants, flowers, shapes, and colors?

_____

_____

_____

_____

_____

_____

_____

_____

» **Write** about a favorite work of art you saw that is nature-based. It could just be loosely related to nature. What did you like about it?

_____

_____

_____

_____

_____

_____

_____

_____

[A COLLAGE WORK INSPIRED BY DUSK, MY FAVORITE TIME OF DAY. I LOVE THE COLORS NATURE SHOWS US DURING THE TRANSITION BETWEEN DAY AND NIGHT.]

 EXERCISE

Gather

» **Collect** shells, seeds, pods, flowers, stones, feathers, or any other objects you find outside that catch your fancy. Bring them home and set them in a special place. Have them serve as a reminder of your experience that day. Arrange them in a way that is visually pleasing to you. You can add other objects, such as fabric, pictures, and fresh flowers, into your little altar space as well. Have this serve as the beginning of your creative altar.

 EXERCISE

Capture

» **Go** out into your city or town and bring a camera, taking photos of everything that inspires you. Slowly make your way into nature nearby, snapping shots along your journey. Print or upload the photos and observe the progression from man-made to natural designs. Make some visual notes of it in your mind. What do you notice? What stands out to you, or what do you find beautiful? If the cityscape still inspires you most, or in equal measure, that is quite all right. This is simply an objective exercise to get you to notice the contrast of both existences.

"Nature is so powerful, so strong. Capturing its essence is not easy—your work becomes a dance with light and the weather. It takes you to a place within yourself."

—ANNIE LEIBOVITZ

[OPPOSITE: A DIGITAL PHOTO SERIES SHOWS A PROGRESSION OF IMAGES, FROM MAN-MADE OBJECTS TO SCENES FROM THE NATURAL WORLD.]

"I'm an introvert ... I love being by myself, love being outdoors, love taking a long walk with my dogs and looking at the trees, flowers, the sky."

—AUDREY HEPBURN

TRY THIS!

» Schedule a day or weekend trip alone to a place in nature you have always wanted to visit. If a trip to the seashore is incredibly restorative for you, find a place near the beach. If you love the deep, misty woods, locate a cabin in the forest. Turn off your cell phone and bring your camera, a sketchbook, colored pens, pencils, an eraser, and a few books or magazines for visual inspiration.

TIP OF THE TRADE

If you need to give your creativity a boost, attending an artist residency can afford you several things. It can give you an allotted amount of time to create a body of work with no outside distractions, while paying very minimal or low rent. It allows you the opportunity to meet and network with other professional artists from around the world. And it can provide a healthy dose of newfound inspiration and ideas, especially because artist residencies are often located in naturally beautiful or rich cultural settings. Check out the websites **www.resartis.org** and **www. artistcommunities.org** for comprehensive residency listings and details on how to apply.

Also, consider treating yourself to a weekend or week-long art retreat or workshop. There are many throughout the world, including workshops I teach at my studio and around the United States at places including Squam Art Workshops in New England and Squam-by-the-Sea on the Outer Banks of North Carolina.

"A leaf fluttered in through the window this morning, as if supported by the rays of the sun, a bird settled on the fire escape, joy in the task of coffee, joy accompanied me as I walked."

—ANAÏS NIN

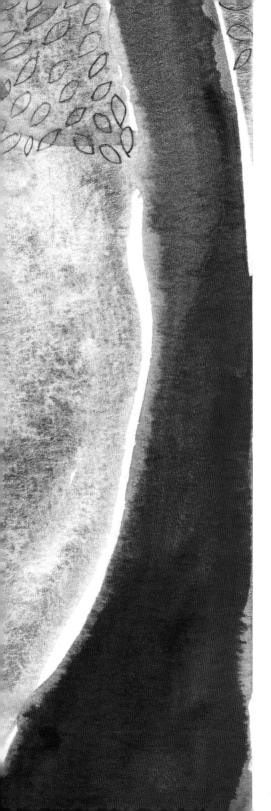

CHAPTER 3

Courting Inspiration

Inspiration is an overused word in the creative field, but its value is endless. Without inspiration, work either does not get done or becomes stagnant.

To keep inspiration itself from getting stagnant, let's think of a few synonyms: *exaltation*, *fancy*, *illumination*, *impulse*, *muse*, *motivation*, *rumble*, *spark*, and *whim*. Just reading that list can send ripples of ideas through me and fill me with a desire to get into the studio.

"Creativity comes from
looking for the unexpected
and stepping outside
your own experience."
—MASARU IBUKA

So, how do you open yourself to inspiration? Taking pleasure in the little things in life can help. Every action can be seen as an act of creation or of love. Washing the dishes while watching the birds dance and the sun stream through the leaves can give you a fresh start to the day. Taking time to sip a cup of coffee on the front porch before heading out can give your mind and heart time and space for cultivating inner riches and illuminating thoughts.

Motivation to create new art springs not only from the little details in life but also from changing up routines. For instance, walking or riding your bike to work instead of getting in the car can unexpectedly push the inspiration button. An object or a person you observe along your walk may generate a whole new set of ideas. Inspiration can even come from noticing the elements alone—such as lines, shapes, or colors.

I love to browse boutiques when I am traveling to get new ideas for color combinations or subjects. For example, John Derian Dry Goods, a charming gift store on the Lower East Side in New York City, always stirs my muse. I might start thinking about using magenta, gray, and a silvery turquoise when I see it on a fabulous embroidered pillow in the window under the glaring streetlights. And then, wait—what about embroidering paintings themselves? I imagine a whole new series of mixed-media paintings with hand-stitched animals and floral motifs on canvas under a heavy gloss. All this occurs because I take an evening stroll outside my hotel to see what other artists, crafters, and designers are making. The possibility for inspiration exists in each moment on Earth, and staying open to those possibilities can ignite whole new worlds within us.

[A TRIP TO A FAVORITE BOUTIQUE CAN BRING IDEAS FOR
NEW COLOR COMBINATIONS OR SUBJECTS.]

Most artists are successful because they work hard and dedicate many hours to their craft. It's a simple rule: An artist who accepts and trusts making art as a full-time pursuit will find more ways to make money from it. The hours spent finding ways to get your work out there along with developing deeper bodies and inventories of work will give you a better chance to support yourself.

But making art as a relaxing hobby is wonderful—and by no means am I dissuading that. In fact, oftentimes it is necessary to do this part-time until things get rolling. I made art on a part time basis for years until things started to break open.

I also happen to believe that the universe responds to effort made, as do people or paying customers. Everything is energy, so the energy you give to your art career will come back in some form. Consistent belief in your efforts helps a great deal, as does laying out varying honeypots. A successful businessperson once told me, "It's valuable to have your hands in as many honeypots as possible in case one of them runs dry." So, find ways to diversify your creativity to make a living while still staying true to your art. Try teaching a workshop, for instance, or selling your work at local craft fairs, or offering your services as a mural painter to local businesses.

Inspiration can run dry at times, and working through the slow periods can help ignite the creative spark again. Numerous times I have felt unmotivated to paint, but because of a deadline, I knew I had to get to it. Then a magical thing happened—as I worked, I became inspired because I was simply in the act of creating. My first works might have appeared scratchy or out of my natural flow, but then something inside me turned on, and I found myself becoming motivated by my own experimentation. I surprised myself by what was coming out of my hand.

I think that is how many artists find stimulation—by working through the blocks and finding ways back into their creative flow.

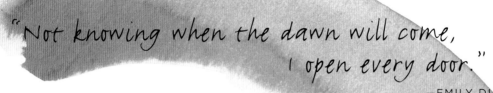

*"Not knowing when the dawn will come,
I open every door."*

—EMILY DICKINSON

[INSPIRATION CAN SOMETIMES BE FOUND JUST OUTSIDE YOUR DOOR. THESE
PHOTOS WERE TAKEN ONE MAGICAL MORNING IN MY NEIGHBORHOOD]

> *"inspiration exists, but it has to find us working."*
>
> —PABLO PICASSO

Courting inspiration requires a combination of earnest dedication to your work and trusting yourself to follow through with what moves you. If, for instance, you fancy geometric shapes and delve deep into the study of sacred geometry, you could create a whole series of works inspired by that. Or if you travel to India and become enthralled by the way people use bright, bold colors, you could begin to build a series based on the patterns and colors you've observed.

Works also can be more narratively structured, based on rich mythologies and stories passed down through time. Rereading favorite fables can be a wonderful way to inspire works that illustrate those stories or help you create modern ones blended with your own mythology. I have always been drawn to the Greek myth of Persephone, who spends her days in nature, planting seeds and looking after plants. When she is abducted by Hades, God of the Underworld, her mother, Demeter, Goddess of the Harvest, is so distraught that she causes a drought. To end the drought, Hades agrees to release Persephone back to her mother, but only if Persephone returns to the Underworld for part of the year. When she is with her mother, the earth is bountiful, but when she is with Hades, it is barren—and thus the seasons came to be.

Although my work doesn't directly relate to this myth, I, too, have my own romantic notions about the seasons, which I like to express in my artwork through colors and lines in many of my trees. Summer and spring can feel like a time of renewal, or a coming together, while winter can sometimes feel like a time to isolate myself from others or retreat to quieter places.

Many artists find inspiration in a desire to correct injustices and help humanity. For instance, an artist might set out to capture world hunger and poverty through a series of jarring photos, or create a performance piece on experiencing a natural disaster with all the consequential repercussions. Through these creations, viewers may feel more emotionally moved to help out or take action.

Motivation to make work may also be part of a healing process where traumatic memories are released and emotional scars transformed into art on the page. Those past stories can then be amended into a new story, one based on your life as you are living it or wish to more fully live it.

Another way to keep inspiration close at hand is to simplify your life. Things that cause you to become distracted are little killers for creativity. Inspiration is more easily courted when your mind is clear and has room to grow. So think of ways to eliminate distractions and streamline your daily existence. One way I make time for myself is to have Internet access only at my studio. I find that I spend so much time on the Internet during the day that it would just be a distraction at night. It helps me create more quiet time for myself when I am at home.

I also like to turn off my phone during times when I meditate, and I spend very little time watching television. When I need some time to unwind, I sometimes take a hot bath using scented bath salts and essential oils or curl up with a good book by candlelight. I also love meeting a dear friend for wine around sunset and then taking a stroll downtown.

"Creativity comes from trust. Trust your instincts. And never hope more than you work." —RITA MAE BROWN

[OTHER CULTURES' USE OF PATTERNS, SHAPES, AND COLORS CAN INFLUENCE WORK IN NEW WAYS.]

"The art of art, the glory of expression and the sunshine of the light of letters, is simplicity." —WALT WHITMAN

"What art offers is space—a certain breathing room for the spirit. —JOHN UPDIKE

 **EXERCISE** # Contemplate

Answer the following questions in your sketchbook:

» **Make a list** of ten things that currently inspire you. They can be anything, from a new song, to that fabulous tapestry coat you just saw in a shop window, to your grandmother's plate collection ... expand your imagination to every corner to gather ideas.

_____   _____

_____   _____

_____   _____

_____   _____

» **Write** about a time when you felt completely inspired or elated—something that really stands out in your memory. What about that experience inspired you? What were the circumstances and where were you in your life? How can you try to create more experiences like that in your life now?

_____

_____

_____

_____

_____

_____

[OPPOSITE: A CHERISHED MEMORY CAN SPAWN A SINGLE OR
A SERIES OF NEW WORK.]

Go Further

How can you simplify your life so that you have more time to work and feel inspired? What things leave you feeling unmotivated or sap your energy? Make a list of those things and see if you can lessen or eliminate them.

_____

_____

_____

_____

_____

_____

_____

_____

_____

_____

_____

_____

_____

_____

EXERCISE Collect & Create

Set aside an area in your studio or home for an inspiration board. The board itself can be made from just about anything—be it corkboard, mat board, cardboard, or canvas. You can include bits of drawings, paintings, photos, or collage on the board. It can address a certain experience in your life or be a collection of various images and things that you love. Draw out words of inspiration with fine marker that solidify and add to the artwork.

[DRIED PLANT MATERIAL OR MAN-MADE OBJECTS CAN BE PART OF AN INSPIRATION BOARD.]

The Elements of Art

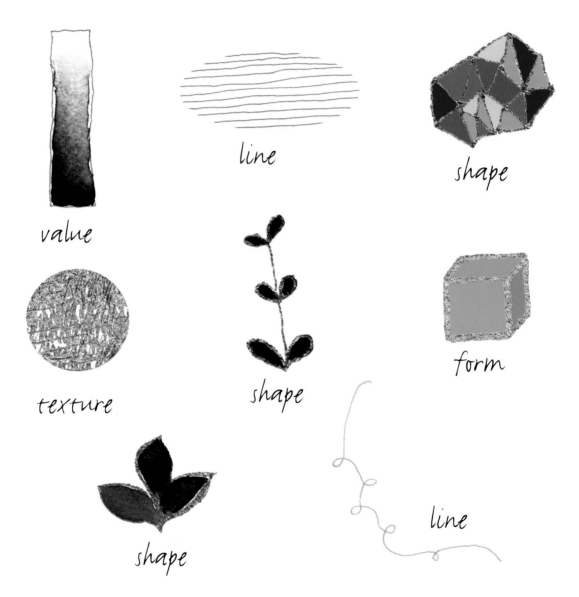

value

line

shape

texture

shape

form

shape

line

[SHOWN HERE ARE THE ELEMENTS OF ART. SOME OR ALL OF THESE ELEMENTS ARE A PART OF EACH WORK OF ART.]

EXERCISE · Collage

Put together a collage of visual elements. Look for colors, textures, lines, shapes, and patterns that move you, and cut them out of books, magazines, and old sketchbooks. Use a variety of different materials for this collage, such as photos, paint, fabric, or objects. Separate the elements if necessary: For example, you can pin different fabrics and textures to the inspiration board, making the whole board itself a collage piece. This is a collage based solely on the elements of art—unlike an inspiration collage, which can be anything.

"Little by little, one walks far."
—PERUVIAN PROVERB

color

[COLOR EXPERIMENTATION IS A VITAL AND POWERFUL ELEMENT IN MANY WORKS OF ART.]

"I found I could say things with color and shapes that I couldn't say any other way—things I had no words for."

—GEORGIA O'KEEFFE

TRY THIS!

» **Shake up your routine** by doing three things this week that are out of the ordinary for you. They can be small or big. For instance, drop into a class you have always wanted to take or experiment in the kitchen by using a new recipe.

» **Dedicate an afternoon** to whet your imagination and get ideas churning. Visit museums, galleries, craft boutiques, or even vintage shops, places that can motivate you to create your own work. Take a long walk in the park afterward and sketch out your ideas.

TIP OF THE TRADE

Consider putting your art on a variety of materials—T-shirts, accessories, wallets, bags, skirts, table runners, pillows, and more. People love things they can touch, wear, and use in a functional way. It may also help you find new niches for your work, draw more customers, and give licensors an idea of how your work translates onto their products. Start out small, both artistically and financially.

Each item you create will need to be photographed well so that it can be showcased on the Web and used for high-resolution prints. Magazines require photos to be in high resolution (300 dpi or greater), and the same applies if you want to make art prints. If you are confident in your skills and have a quality camera, take photographs yourself. If not, consider hiring a friend; perhaps he or she will do it as a trade for some of your items. I have traded with numerous photographers for art goods or services.

You can make art prints either open or limited-edition and on archival paper or even mounted on wood panels. Having prints makes your original artwork more valuable because there is only one original but a hundred prints of that same image.

Aesthetic consistency woven throughout all your lines is important, too. This helps people recognize your work and makes it feel symbiotic. I like to experiment with my work and never want to limit new ideas, but I find that people can understand me better as an artist when I have certain visual themes woven throughout.

[HERE IS A SNAPSHOT OF MY ART ON ORGANIC SCARVES AND SHAWLS, ALONG WITH PRINTS IN RECYCLED BARN WOOD FRAMES AND ORIGINALS ON WOOD AND CANVAS.]

CHAPTER 4

Enriching Patterns

A motif is a dominant element or decorative pattern in art. Just as in life, in art we may be attracted to certain motifs or patterns. Noticing these patterns and being aware of how they affect us can be helpful for our personal growth.

Some patterns can be detrimental to the spirit, while others move us forward creatively and help us live healthy lives. Certainly, there is comfort in routine. For instance, every morning after I get out of bed, I like to make a cup of green tea with honey—hot or iced, depending on the season.

[THE HALOED BIRD IS A MOTIF THAT I HAVE USED IN SEVERAL PAINTINGS.]

"To understand is to perceive patterns." —ISAIAH BERLIN

[A PARTICULAR MOTIF CAN SPAWN IDEAS FOR A SERIES OF WORK.]

> *"Things start out as hopes and end up as habits."*
> —LILLIAN HELLMAN

I then take my dog out for a short walk and sit on a park bench with my cup of tea. Slowly I begin to wake up as I watch my dog play. The surrounding sounds of morning traffic combined with birdsong gradually heighten my senses and get me going. If I have some extra time, I will practice yoga and catch up on phone calls at home.

I know many other people who follow specific routines when they awake or before they fall sleep. One of my friends always makes a cup of home-made chai with dried herbs as he wakes, while another writes in her journal and reads passages from devotional books to start every morning anew.

Patterns are not solely action-based. Some are mental and emotional and can lead to repetitive actions, or hinder us from making changes. Recognizing and changing negative thought patterns can be a stimulant for new ideas and experiences in life.

[TRY CREATING A MOVING MOTIF THAT GRADUALLY CHANGES OR TRANSFORMS.]

 **EXERCISE** # My Habits

In a stream-of-consciousness fashion (i.e., without think-ing too much), jot down a list of your daily or weekly habits. Do not judge whether these are good or bad, just make note of actions you see yourself frequently repeat-ing. Write down mental and emotional habits as well as actions. For instance, what repeated thoughts do you have throughout the week? What emotional responses do you have to them?

After your list is done, mark the habits you want to change. Draw lines from each of those and replace them with new habits you can see yourself taking on. Try elimi-nating one disempowering habit by replacing it with a favorable one that can enhance your life. This is a tool for transforming patterns in our lives.

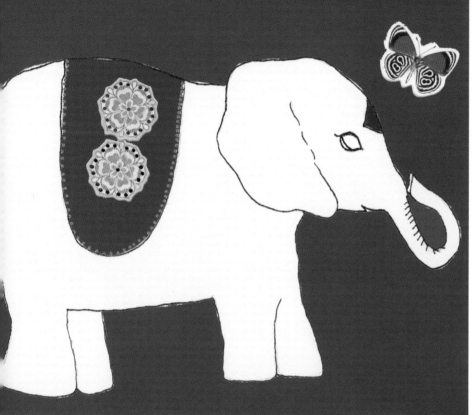

Frequent sketching and observing can help us understand what patterns we are drawn to. I love to spend hours browsing in bookstores. Sometimes I look through books that contain ancient symbols. I also spend time in the art history section to see what sort of motifs artists from other eras have used. Gustav Klimt's work enthralls me with its repetition of gold spirals, which fuse into a rich tapestry solidly blanketing his ethereal subjects.

"Habits change into character." —OVID

[TRY PAINTING A SINGLE SUBJECT IN DIFFERENT WAYS AND WITH DIFFERENT MEDIA.]

In this way, art can be a practice that brings new patterns or motifs. Those motifs may run through an entire body of work. Perhaps a certain style of painting circles or lines, or a particular subject matter like circus animals or vintage botanicals, becomes a thread that links works together.

"Art is pattern informed by sensibility." —HERBERT READ

"Diligence is the mother of good fortune." —BENJAMIN DISRAELI

I have found that my attitude and work ethic are everything in my art career. The steadier I become in my practice of creativity, the more I benefit.

To stay focused, I try to eliminate unproductive distractions, like becoming sidetracked by negativity or overly discouraged by setbacks. If someone makes a destructive comment about my work, I try not to allow this to disrupt my process, but rather simply take note of it and move on.

Professional setbacks will happen, as will getting your hopes up only to have them brought down. *Good Morning America*, *Martha Stewart*, and the *Oprah Winfrey Show* have all contacted me about featuring my work, but it has never made the final cut. Talk about disappointment! But you must persist, move forward, and trust that you will have another opportunity like that again. The powers of believing in and loving what you do are incredible resources to have.

Finding joy in your work—becoming excited about the possibilities with each new piece—keeps you diligent.

A way to keep the spark in the studio is through experimentation. I know several artists who complain about being "stuck" in their style because they feel they have to be consistent in order to keep their patrons happy or to stay successful. But I think staying current and true to your own aesthetics will keep you successful. This doesn't mean that personal motifs are abandoned; having a recognizable thread throughout your work is essential. But staying curious and trying something new helps you stay excited about your creative process.

For example, experimentation with a new medium can open up new worlds. What if you discover you are a natural with watercolor? Or that adding an encaustic or resin surface to your paintings gives them a depth that they so unexpectedly needed? Along with implementing new habits in your life, try adding one new element or technique to your artwork.

[OPPOSITE TOP: FOCUSING ON A SINGLE ELEMENT IN A FAVORITE WORK OF ART CAN SPARK NEW WAYS OF MAKING WORK. KLIMT'S GOLDEN SPIRALS INSPIRED THIS SIMPLE WATERCOLOR.]

[OPPOSITE BELOW: TRY USING FAVORITE PERSONAL MOTIFS IN NEW WAYS. I LOVE TO PAINT PEACOCKS, SO IN THIS PAINTING I PLACED A PART OF A PEACOCK FEATHER ON A FOX'S FOREHEAD.]

"Failure happens all the time. It happens every day in practice. What makes you better is how you react to it." —MIA HAMM

EXERCISE Reflect

Write about the following in your sketchbook:

» What patterns have you witnessed throughout your life? Look back into childhood and write down anything you have repeatedly observed. How did it make you feel?

_____

_____

_____

_____

_____

_____

_____

» Which of these patterns are still taking place now? They can be as simple as the fact that you loved to dance as a child and still do. Or that your family had certain habits that you know did not benefit you, but because they were so frequently observed, you have now taken them up yourself. Take time to reflect on this.

EXERCISE Create

» Summarize what you have just written down and make a list of your favorite habits. Turn each of these into visual representations; they can be as literal or abstract as you would like. Get ideas from looking through books on symbols or your collages from previous exercises. Sketch out each motif until you feel happy. It's okay if you come up with just a few motifs.

» Use your favorite motif to create a simple, small art series. Try using varying color combinations or line qualities. Express the motif in a different fashion or style for each work of art.

Go Further

Carve your personal motif into a rubber stamp so that you can use it on packaging or press materials. If you do not want to carve it, you can scan your motif and upload it to a custom stamp website, such as Simon's Stamps (www.simonstamp.com/).

[HERE IS A STAMP I ORDERED FROM A DRAWING I MADE. I USE THIS STAMP ALONG WITH OTHERS ON VARIOUS MATERIALS, INCLUDING ENVELOPES, PACKAGES, AND TAGS.]

"It is your work in life that is the ultimate seduction." —PABLO PICASSO

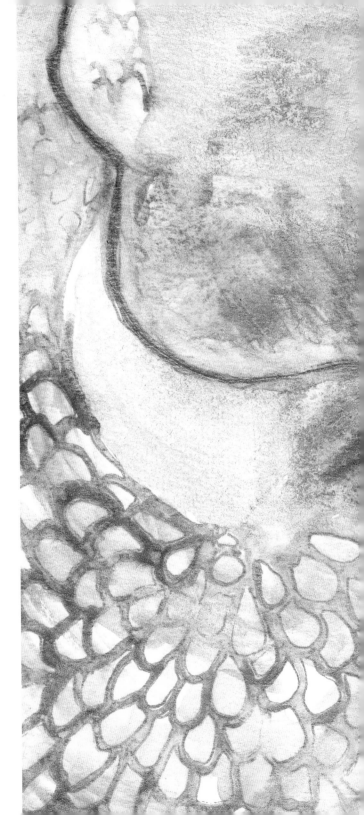

TRY THIS!

» Set a schedule for your art making. Write down in your datebook the hours you will devote to making art. Don't take on too much at first; start out small and slowly build.

» Make artful things and experimentation a part of your daily existence. Try rearranging your furniture or décor in your home. Buy deliciously scented handmade soaps for both your shower and kitchen, along with some fresh flowers. Go thrift or boutique shopping and buy something that feels daring, whether it's a shiny new dress, long feather earrings, or a silly printed tee. Paint your nails bright red. Try things out of the norm that enliven the artist within you.

[OPPOSITE: MY WORK OFTEN USES NATURAL FORMS AND BO-
TANICALS IN A LINEAR FASHION. I REPEATEDLY USE UPRIGHT
SEED FORMS OR STEMS, AS SEEN IN BETWEEN THE PRESSED
ORCHIDS. NATURE USED IN A MINIMAL STYLE SYMBOLIZES
PEACE AND TRANQUILITY IN MY WORK.]

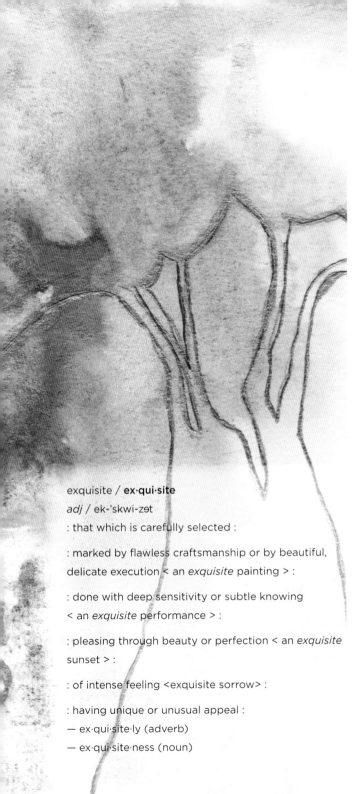

exquisite / **ex·qui·site**

adj / ek-ˈskwi-zət

: that which is carefully selected :

: marked by flawless craftsmanship or by beautiful, delicate execution < an *exquisite* painting > :

: done with deep sensitivity or subtle knowing < an *exquisite* performance > :

: pleasing through beauty or perfection < an *exquisite* sunset > :

: of intense feeling <exquisite sorrow> :

: having unique or unusual appeal :

— ex·qui·site·ly (adverb)

— ex·qui·site·ness (noun)

TIP OF THE TRADE

Create a personal story to connect to your work. To stand out in a crowd, you need something unique in your style and artistic mission. What do you ultimately want to share with the world? Do you have a message, or is your work simply about technique or beauty? Through experimentation and practice this becomes evident. Write a statement and have some friends and family give you feedback. Weave that personal aesthetic and mission through your work.

Design several logos that you can use on your business cards, postcards, and website. Make your business cards feel special. Maybe you would like yours hand-printed, letter-pressed, or cut in a unique shape, such as a square instead of a rectangle. I have opted for rounded corners for years, which I find nicely complement my aesthetic.

sketch some logo ideas

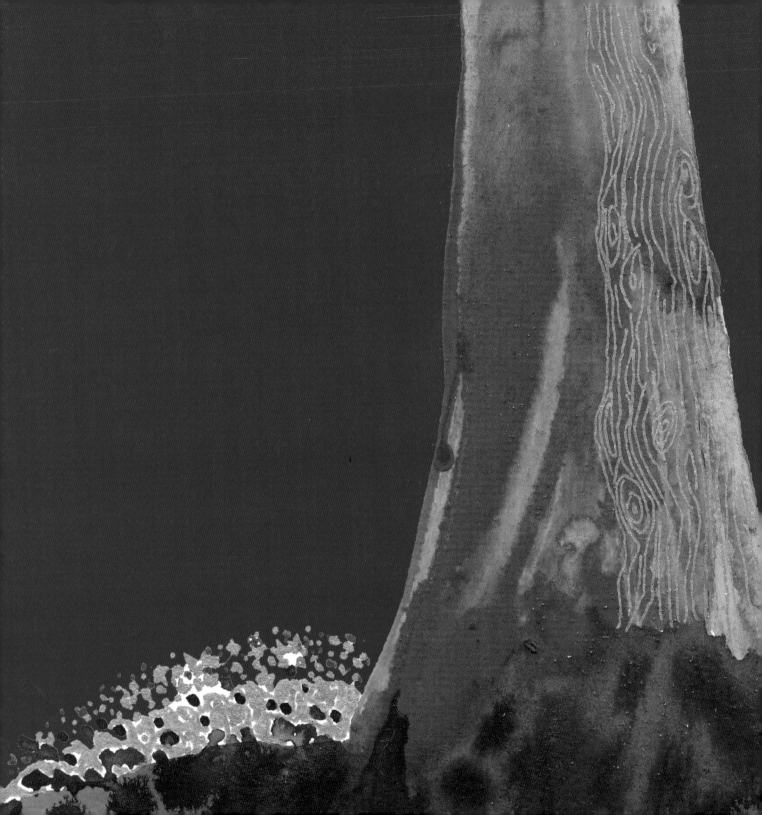

CHAPTER 5

Herbal Lore

Artists sometimes have a tendency to neglect their health. We can become so absorbed in our work that we neglect our bodies. I have seen artists who live in studios without sufficient heat, or who feed themselves with coffee and cigarettes. This sounds terribly cliché, and is by no means universal. Yet some people who thrive on self-expression also harbor unnecessarily romantic ideas about artistic self-sacrifice. Or they may simply lack the cash flow to properly take care of themselves. But when a life is lived in balance and good health, creativity and success will more easily to follow.

[MOTHER NATURE'S FLOWERS AND
PLANTS CAN PROVIDE NUTRITIONAL
AND MEDICINAL SUPPORT.]

"After tea it's back to painting—a large poplar
at dusk with a gathering storm."

—GUSTAV KLIMT

Wellness and healing start with Mother Nature. Plant remedies for focus, longevity, and inspiration have existed for thousands of years in many cultures. They have been passed on by word of mouth, by written text, and through rituals.

The plant nettle, popularly known for its sting when touched, is a favorite among herbalists because it is so nutrient-rich, containing vitamins A and C and a great deal of minerals. And the herb schisandra, which the Chinese revere, seems to be good for just about anything—from helping the mind focus to making the skin radiant.

So, partaking in a warm cup of herbal tea is both a lovely ritual and a nice way to focus your senses before a long day of art making.

"God sleeps in the minerals, awakens in plants, walks in animals, and thinks in man."
—ARTHUR YOUNG

[NATURE CAN HOLD VAST INTRICACIES AND WORKINGS.]

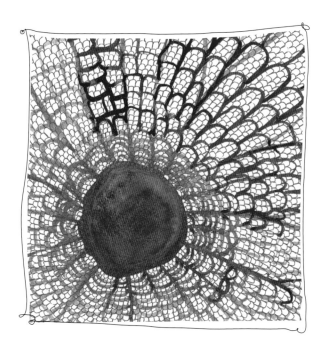

This section details a selection of herbs that may be used to help stimulate creativity, treat certain ailments, or support overall wellness. You can typically find them in the bulk section of a health food store or at a local apothecary.

To make a tea infusion, add a heaping teaspoon of herbs for every cup of water in a cooking pot. Bring the water just to a boil and then immediately turn off the heat. Let the herbs soak, covered, for five to ten minutes, and then strain. Pour the tea into a tall stainless steel cup or a glass jar container, like a Mason jar. Sweeten with honey if desired and sip throughout the day for creative and nutritional sustenance.

If making tea seems too time-consuming, you can also buy herbs in a tincture (or alcohol-based) formula. Simply add the specified number of drops as written on the label to warm water or juice.

"Energy is eternal delight."
—WILLIAM BLAKE

"Health is my expected heaven."
—JOHN KEATS

Herbs for Creative Stimulation

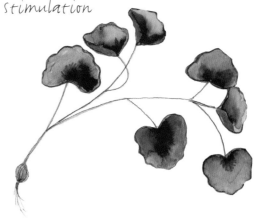

GINGKO BILOBA, one of the oldest living trees in the world, is known to improve cognitive function, providing focus and clear thinking. The leaves in particular are thought to help with memory and circulating blood flow to the brain.

GOTU KOLA, which originated in the East and has been used in homeopathic medicine for many centuries, is another brain herb, increasing mental abilities and concentration as well as easing anxiety.

MUGWORT, associated with the Greek goddess Artemis and the moon, enhances the subconscious, making dreams more colorful. Artemis is known to send celestial dreams to those who call on her. Mugwort has often been used in various spiritual rituals to ward off evil spirits or bad energies. It is also said to enhance one's intuitive abilities. I have noticed that drinking a cup of mugwort before bedtime or even leaving a few dried leaves under my pillow has induced more vivid dreaming.

GREEN TEA is rich in antioxidants and helps protect your body from free radicals, or destructive molecules. I love to drink a cup of green tea pearls with jasmine right before I paint. It gives me a clear, energetic feeling and focus with just enough caffeine to help stimulate my creative sensibilities.

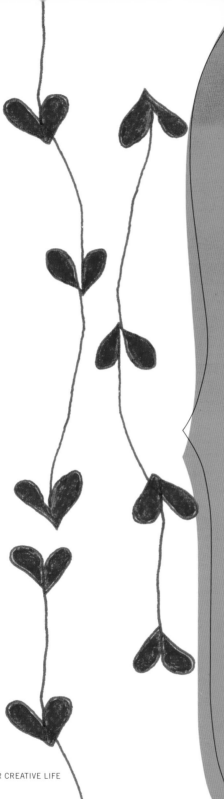

Herbs for the immune system

PAU D'ARCO, an herb native to South America, may help boost the immune system and treat certain pathologies, like the flu and some bacterial infections. The herb comes from a large canopy tree native to the Amazon rainforest. For hundreds of years, indigenous tribal people of the Amazon would use it for medicinal purposes. The Inca thought the tree had godlike qualities.

GOLDEN SEAL was first introduced to Western society by Native American tribes, and is often used as a natural antibiotic and may help treat cold and flu symptoms and upset stomachs. The Cherokee tribe in particular used it for digestive disorders and as an antibacterial eyewash. Today it is commonly used to treat upper respiratory infections.

REISHi, a mushroom revered in Eastern medicine for its ability to increase immunity and ward off disease, is what I like to take when I begin to feel ill with a cold or allergies. It can also reduce inflammation and calm the nerves. It's more or less a wonder mushroom!

Draw Your Favorite Herbs and Flowers:

RED CLOVER, a nutrient-rich herb that also acts as a blood purifier, may help cleanse the liver and rid the body of excess mucus. The herb grows abundantly in meadows where I live, and I like to pick the clover bud right in the wild and eat a few just for nutritional sustenance.

"I do not yet know why plants come out of the land or float in streams, or creep on rocks or roll from the sea. I am entranced by the mystery of them, and absorbed by their variety and kinds. Everywhere they are visible yet everywhere occult."

—LIBERTY HYDE BAILEY

Herbs for Insomnia

CHAMOMILE, a popular herb, is a mild sedative that's helpful for relaxing nerves. The Egyptians revered it over all other herbs and dedicated it to their sun god. Due to its sedative qualities, it was used in some love potions during the Middle Ages.

HOPS can ease insomnia when nothing else seems to work. Along with calming the nervous system, it may also help reduce pain and inflammation. I often place one dried hop flower in a teacup and pour hot water over it. I sip it just before bedtime while reading for a peaceful sleep.

VALERIAN has been used since ancient Greek and Roman times to quell insomnia and relieve anxiety. Drink the tea one hour before bedtime, or throughout the day if needed. Do not drink more than three cups a day. Some people may have an adverse reaction to valerian, so try just a small cup at first.

Herbs for Overall Support

NETTLE is a rich source of vitamins, minerals, and amino acids, including calcium, iron, magnesium, and potassium. It helps sustain energy levels and strengthens bones, teeth, skin, and hair. Nettle is the main herb I take for alleviating seasonal allergies.

OATSTRAW, a nutrient-rich herb that increases energy and provides nourishment for vital organs, is specifically known to help teeth, bones, skin, and hair. It's best to drink oatstraw over a consistent time period to fully receive the benefits.

SCHISANDRA, a star herb in Chinese medicine, helps keep the mind and memory sharp, replenishes kidney energy, cleanses the liver, and revitalizes skin. I love to take schisandra in a tincture form. I notice that it gives me focus and a subtle energy boost.

"You can't get a cup of tea big enough or a book long enough to suit me."

—C.S. LEWIS

[SCHISANDRA (MAGNOLIA VINE)]

Herbs for stress

HOLY BASIL, known as tulsi in India, is a favorite stress-reducing herb that is revered in Ayurvedic medicine. Holy basil is also said to help increase stamina and regulate blood sugar levels. I love making a warm chai latte with tulsi during the winter months. I find it keeps my body warm and energized. Holy basil is medicinal in quality, while commercial basil is more commonly used for cooking.

PASSIONFLOWER is an intricate and gorgeous flower with ten petals and sepals. It is another well-known calming herb that helps relax the nervous system and treat irritability. It is particularly effective when blended with other herbs. Ancient Aztec and Peruvian cultures used passionflower for medicinal purposes. When the Spanish discovered the flower and brought it back to Europe, it became known for its sedative qualities.

LEMON BALM, also known as melissa, is another personal favorite. It has been used since the Middle Ages to help ease stress and anxiety. Just-picked lemon balm can also be a refreshing supplement to a cool drink during warmer months.

SKULLCAP, used among Cherokee and other Native American tribes, is known to promote a sense of calm and may help with anxiety or nervous tension. It also has antispasmodic qualities and may relieve muscle cramps.

FLOWER ESSENCES are another natural remedy touted for their artistic benefits. They were first created by Dr. Edward Bach, a homeopath who lived in England during the early 1900s and spent much time in the woods studying the particular qualities of different flowers. A "vibrational" form of plant medicine, flower essences are made by a solar infusion process in which flowers soak in water in full sunlight to transmit their unique energetic signatures. Each energetic flower signature can help ease a variety of mental or emotional distresses. You can now find flower essence blends at almost any health food store, and some, like iris and Indian paintbrush, are known to specifically help with creativity. I have several artist friends who swear by them, and I myself have felt benefits from taking certain blends, such as larch and sagebrush. Flower essences can be ingested up to four times daily, with a few drops placed on the tongue each time. Or you can add two to four drops to a glass of drinking water and sip the mixture throughout the day.

"The intense perfumes of the wild herbs as we trod them underfoot made us feel almost drunk."
—JACQUELINE DU PRÉ

"One of the most attractive things about the flowers is their beautiful reserve."
—HENRY DAVID THOREAU

suggested Flower Essence Blends

ALOE VERA is good for people who are burned out from too much activity. It can help center and integrate creativity into one's being.

BLACKBERRY is a willpower blend to help bring artists' ideas into the world.

LARCH removes any stifled feelings and helps instinctual creative expression flow.

SAGEBRUSH helps eliminate fixed concepts and brings fresh perception and original ideas.

SHASTA DAISY helps with synthesizing numerous creative ideas into a meaningful singular work.

YELLOW STAR tulip inspires compassion and empathy in the artist that may subsequently show up in his or her work.

INDIAN PAINTBRUSH helps restore and replenish physical vitality so that it flows into creative inspiration.

BUTTERCUP, a self-esteem blend, helps artists understand the value of their work.

IRIS, perhaps the best-known flower essence for creative pursuits, helps with transcending into higher realms of expression.

 **EXERCISE** # Reflect

Answer the following questions in your sketchbook:

» In what ways do you feel your health could improve? Write out some goals for improving your health in the coming months and year. Write down some tangible steps to make that happen.

» How do you think your art would change if you felt more vital? Don't be afraid of what comes up; just envision what this would look like. Draw some sketches or ideas. If you feel it wouldn't change much, write about why you think so.

Vital to Your Life

"*Health is the greatest gift, contentment the greatest wealth, faithfulness the best relationship.*"

—BUDDHA

 **EXERCISE** # Construct

» Make a dream pillow using the dream herb mugwort.

You can create your own pillow by cutting out two squares (around 7-inches [17.8 cm]-wide on each side) from a silky fabric. Sew three sides together. Find a mesh bag and fill it with mugwort and any other herbs of your choice. Rose petals or lavender, for example, are pleasantly aromatic and also calming. To further enhance vivid dreaming, add mint or orange peel. For lucid dreaming, try adding a few drops of essential oils such as clary sage or anise. Sew the last side together to close the bag. You can decorate the fabric beforehand with fabric pens or sew a special piece of fabric to one or both of the sides.

 **EXERCISE** # Make

» Make your own specialized flower essence blend in a small glass jar.

Flower essences are made by a process of dilution. I find it's best to combine no more than five individual flower essences to make your own personal blend. To make a combination blend, purchase a small dropper bottle at a health food store and add a few drops of each essence to it. Fill one-quarter of the bottle with brandy or apple cider vinegar and distilled water.

Go Further

Keep a health or plant diary. Note what teas or flower essences you have been taking and any changes in your health that may have resulted. From this process, you can begin to discover which plants are your allies. Friends of mine who study herbs and flower essences often have unique bonds with certain types.

If the herbal world is not calling you, just keep a health diary. Notice how you feel after you consume certain foods and drinks and make note of it. Jot down how much sleep you get each day, too. See if you become aware of any patterns.

To make your own essence from scratch, find a flower you feel called to and let the petals and buds (sans stems and leaves) soak in a glass bowl with water in full sunlight for three to four hours. Pour the water and a half amount of brandy or apple cider vinegar into a small glass bottle or jar. This is called the mother tincture. Add a few drops from the mother tincture and place in a small glass bottle with one-third brandy or vinegar and two-thirds distilled water. This is the stock bottle. Several drops are then added from the stock to the final bottle, called the dosage bottle, which again has a small amount of brandy or vinegar filled with water. Create your own label for each and distinguish with a little intention or description on the dosage bottle.

"There must be quite a few things that a hot bath won't cure, but I don't know any of them." –

SYLVIA PLATH

TRY THIS!

» Take a tea bath just before bedtime. Find some relaxing and sweet-smelling herbs such as lavender, hops, rose petals, or calendula. Place the herbs in a mesh sachet that can be tied shut, and drop the sachet into the tub when the hot water is running. Let the tea bag soak the whole time you bathe, squeezing it every so often.

» Buy some fresh herbs of your choosing from a local farmers' market and make your own tincture—a real pleasure. Place the herbs in a glass container and pour a high-content grain alcohol over them. Let the herbs soak for a few days on a windowsill, shaking the container every once in a while. Strain the plant material and use the alcohol formula as plant medicine. Add one or two tablespoons a day to warm water or juice.

TIP OF THE TRADE

Each of us has a unique understanding of and knowledge about the world. For instance, besides making art, I love studying plant spirit medicine. Use your passions to create a class in your local area. Also share your knowledge online through various social-networking sites, your website, or a blog. This can complement and enhance your creative work. Contact art retreats or centers and offer a workshop in your area of expertise. We each have a gift to share with the world.

ideas:

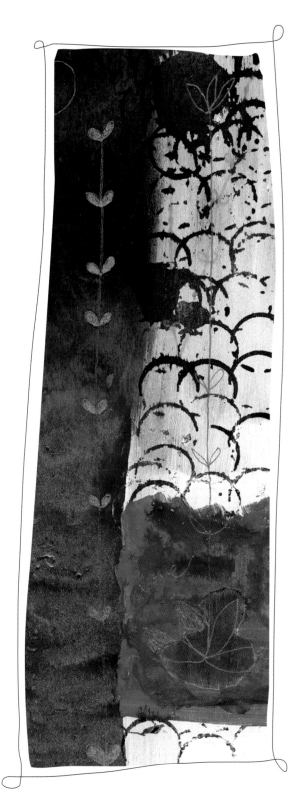

"Passion is energy.
Feel the power that
comes from focusing on
what excites you."

—OPRAH WINFREY

"For breath is life, and if you breathe well, you will live long on Earth."

—SANSKRIT PROVERB

CHAPTER 6

Breathing Deep

Yoga is an art form that has existed in India for thousands of years. It consists of many methodologies, from physical postures to yogic philosophy. I have found that yoga and art making work together very harmoniously, especially in the sense that yoga is a tool to open up the channels that allow more energy to flow.

I first discovered yoga about fifteen years ago, when I was in my early twenties and a junior in college. The class was offered at my university's gym, and I remember the room being full of people. As the class was winding down and we were all lying on our backs in total relaxation pose, or Savasana, I noticed a shift in my being. I felt so much lighter, mentally, emotionally, and physically, as if I had unwound parts of my body that had never been unwound before.

I knew then this was a practice I'd keep for life.

[YOGA POSES, OR *ASANAS*, HAVE BEEN PRACTICED FOR THOUSANDS OF YEARS TO ATTAIN CLARITY AND SERENITY. SHOWN HERE IS WARRIOR I POSE, ALSO KNOWN AS *VIRABHADRASANA I*.]

"A human being is only breath and shadow."
—SOPHOCLES

[AS CLOUDS PASS AND SEASONS CHANGE, I FIND MORE AND MORE THAT BREATH IS MY ANCHOR.]

"What can we do but keep
on breathing in and out,
modest and willing, and in
our places?" —MARY OLIVER

Throughout the years I have explored many styles of yoga, from a gentle or beginner-type class to more advanced styles of *Jivamukti* and *Ashtanga*. Yoga has been helpful for my creative process because it allows me to take care of parts of my body that feel overworked, while at the same time drawing me into my center, away from the chatter of my mind and into my instinctual and intuitive self. A dedication to this type of practice helps my creativity flow more easily and gracefully.

In Sanskrit, the word prana means "life force" or "energy." *Pranayama* means to control the life force, which can be done through breathing techniques. A naturally flowing, unrestrained breath may help calm the nervous system and unify the mind-body connection as well as ease and relax tension in the body. Healthy and conscious breath control can also help the body's digestive and circulatory systems. *Pranayama* may also help tone the muscles and nerves of the internal organs, as well as increase oxygen in the bloodstream.

Creative people of all types can benefit from learning *pranayama* techniques to feel more grounded as well as nourish their spirits. To practice *pranayama*, wear loose-fitting clothes and seek out a quiet space in your home or garden where you can sit comfortably.

"Feelings come and go like clouds in a windy sky. Conscious breathing is my anchor." —THICH NHAT HANH

PRANAYAMA TECHNIQUES

Samavrtti means "same action" or "turning" and focuses on each inhalation and exhalation being equal in quality and duration. *Samavrtti* breathing can be a foundation for every other *pranayama* practice, where the focus is also on having a natural flow from each inhalation to exhalation. Begin to practice this by counting each inhalation and exhalation until the rhythm and quality of the breath seem even.

Ujjayi translates to "victorious breath" and is commonly practiced during an active yoga class. To perform *Ujjayi pranayama*, direct each breath to the back of the throat by slowly inhaling through the nose and exhaling through a wide-open mouth. Create a soft hissing "ha" sound that almost sounds like the ocean. This wavelike sound will begin to come naturally with a little practice. The sound signifies how well and even the breath is flowing, and keeps you aware of taking breaths at regular intervals during physical exertion.

Deergha Swasam, or "three-part breath," is done by breathing in a wavelike motion from the pelvic region to the upper chest. Try this by lying on your back with your knees bent. With your hands on your lower belly, inhale so that your hands rise. Next, draw the inhalation up your torso to the mid-belly—expanding the rib cage—and finally to the upper chest. Allow the exhalation to reverse in the same fashion from the chest down to the belly, with the navel being drawn back to the spine.

Kapalabhati, or "skull-brightener breath," helps increase circulation and energy and is also thought of as a way to cleanse the body's internal systems. Sit in a cross-legged position and place your hands on top of your lower abdomen. In a rapid pace, contract your belly with each exhalation so that the air is forced out through the lungs and the nose. Inhalations will naturally occur after each exhalation, with the exhalations active and the inhalations passive (meaning that exhalations will be consciously executed, while inhalations effortlessly follow each exhalation). Do these eight or so times until you feel comfortable. Once you have gotten the technique down, do twenty-five to thirty exhalations. With practice you can do 100 or more cycles in each sitting.

Many more *pranayama* techniques can be practiced while doing poses, or *asanas*. A steady yoga practice of flowing or seated asanas helps me loosen and unwind my shoulders and neck, which often get tense from the repetitive movement of art making and time on the computer. I have found throughout the years that certain asanas are specifically beneficial for me as a working artist who at times can get a little stressed with deadlines.

"Blessed are the flexible, for they shall not be bent out of shape."
—AUTHOR UNKNOWN

[PRACTICE *PRANAYAMA* BY WEARING COMFORTABLE CLOTHING. YOU CAN SIT IN A CROSS-LEGGED POSITION AND ELEVATE YOUR HIPS JUST ABOVE YOUR KNEES BY SITTING ON A PILLOW.]

ASANAS FOR ARTISTS

Neck rolls: Sit in a comfortable seated position with your spine straight and shoulders relaxed. Take a few deep breaths in and out and close your eyes. Begin to roll your neck gently to the right side, allowing your chin to come close to your chest in the center until it rolls back to the left side. Take a pause and then repeat the motion in the opposite direction. Do this several times with a slow and consistent breath (practice *Samavrtti pranayama* if you'd like). If there are any places of tension, simply hold your neck in that spot and breathe into the tight area for several seconds (I especially love that part).

Shoulder rolls: Continuing in a seated position, sit with your spine straight and chin parallel to the floor. As you inhale, lift and tense your shoulders up toward your ears, and then quickly exhale and release your shoulders down completely. Repeat this for several minutes. Also try rolling your shoulders backward and forward with a steady flow of inhalations for the lift and exhalations for the release.

Bharadvajasana, or Seated Twist, is a simple pose that can help release tension in your neck, shoulders, and spine. With your legs stretched in front of you, swing them just outside your left hip with your knees bent and your weight shifted to your right buttock. Inhale and begin to twist to the right, soften your belly, and keep your hips on the floor. Place your left hand on your right knee and lay your right hand just beside your right hip. Continue to twist to the right, pulling your left shoulder back while turning your head in the same direction to look over your right shoulder. As you inhale, lift your sternum and with each exhalation see if you can twist back a little deeper. Stay in this twist for up to one minute, then shift your shoulders and hips and twist on the other side for the same length of time to balance out your body.

Gomukhasana, or Cow Face Pose: This is a wonderful stretch for the shoulders, triceps, and chest. Start out by sitting in a cross-legged position, and then place your right knee over your left so that both knees are stacked atop each other and your ankles are near both of your hips and on the floor. Find an even balance sitting in this position with your ankles equidistant from both hips. Inhale and stretch both arms out from your sides, parallel to the floor. Draw your right arm behind your torso and tuck it so that your forearm is parallel to your waist. Next, move the back of your right hand between your shoulder blades. Now, inhale and lift your left arm straight above your head, bend your elbow, and place your hand on your back to grab your right hand if possible. You can also use a sock or yoga strap for both hands to grab onto. Breathe in and out for one minute, into any places of tension, and then switch your position entirely so that your legs and arms are now in reverse. Hold the position for the same length of time.

Adho Mukha Svanasana, or Downward-Facing Dog Pose: Probably the most well-known asana in yoga, this is a wonderful pose to energize the body and stretch out numerous parts, including the shoulders, calves, and hamstrings. Begin by coming to the floor on your hands and knees, with your hips directly over your knees. Place your hands in front of your shoulders and outstretch your palms. Exhale and lift your hips, making sure your toes turn under so that they are flat on the floor. Have your knees slightly bent and your heels lifted just off the floor. Raise your sitting bones up toward the ceiling, straightening your knees but not locking them. Try bringing your heels down to the floor as much as you can, without forcing them down. Your arms are strong and straight, with palms and fingers firmly pressed to the floor. Hold this position and breathe there for one to three minutes.

Uttana Shishosana, or Extended Puppy Pose: This is a favorite asana of mine to stretch the shoulders and back. Bring yourself onto all fours on the floor so that your shoulders are above your wrists and your hips are above your knees. Walk your hands forward in front of you, and curl your toes under and exhale as you bring your buttocks back toward your feet. Bring your head to the floor and breathe deeply as your body unwinds and relaxes. Stretch your arms straight in front of you, while keeping your elbows fairly straight, and press your hands down on the floor and pull your hips back. Breathe here for up to a minute and then release.

This list only gives a handful of examples; there are many more yoga poses to try that provide numerous benefits. For instance, just simply touching my toes while standing is nice to get the blood flowing in the other direction and release tension from my back. I also like to sit on the floor and lean over my legs and touch my toes, or lie on my back and bring my knees to my chest and rock gently from side to side.

End every yoga sequence by lying in *Savasana*, a complete relaxtion pose with your back on the floor, which helps the body integrate all the benefits and deeply calms the nervous system. Be mindful to do all the poses gently and with focus on the breath while paying special attention to delicate areas of the body, such as the neck, knees, and spine. Never push yourself beyond your means. Little by little, great things will come.

[TOP RIGHT: BREATHE SLOWLY AND DEEPLY AS YOUR ROLL YOUR NECK FROM SIDE TO SIDE. PRACTICE NECK ROLLS AS A WAY TO TAKE MINI-BREAKS FROM ART MAKING OR COMPUTER TIME.]

[MIDDLE RIGHT: SITTING IN A COMFORTABLE POSITION, TWIST TO BOTH THE LEFT AND THE RIGHT TO LOOSEN YOUR SPINE AND RELEASE STRESS. }

[BELOW RIGHT: THIS SIMPLE STRETCH OF THE SHOULDERS, WHICH SHOULD BE DONE ON EACH SIDE, IS A NICE BALANCE AFTER DOING *GOMUKHASANA*, OR COW FACE POSE.]

Ah, *meditation*—a word that holds much stigma and resistance, and yet, perhaps, also possibility and intrigue. I have found meditation to be one of the most valuable and significant tools for sculpting my existence. It is the time that I get to rest inside, as I'm drawn into my center and away from life's daily distractions and responsibilities.

Many yoga and spiritual centers offer meditation instruction and time and space to practice sitting. I like to believe that the perfect teacher or class will appear just as you are ready, so it's helpful to keep your eyes and mind open for that opportunity.

Any of the *pranayama* techniques mentioned earlier can be practiced before meditation, to prepare the mind and body for silence.

Meditation can be a simple time to sit in stillness with your eyes closed and spine straight, but with your body completely relaxed. To begin, carve out a quiet time to sit in a chair or cross-legged on the floor with a pillow under your hips, and place your palms on your knees or relax them gently in your lap. You may want to wrap a blanket around you if you tend to get cold.

"Meditation is the soul's perspective glass."

—OWEN FELTHAM

"Last Night, as I Was Sleeping"

Last night, as I was sleeping,
I dreamt—marvelous error!—
that a spring was breaking
out in my heart.
I said: Along which secret aqueduct,
Oh water, are you coming to me,
water of a new life
that I have never drunk?

Last night, as I was sleeping,
I dreamt—marvelous error!—
that I had a beehive
here inside my heart.
And the golden bees
were making white combs
and sweet honey
from my old failures.

Last night, as I was sleeping,
I dreamt—marvelous error!—
that a fiery sun was giving
light inside my heart.
It was fiery because I felt
warmth as from a hearth,
and sun because it gave light
and brought tears to my eyes.

Last night, as I slept,
I dreamt—marvelous error!—
that it was God I had
here inside my heart.

—ANTONIO MACHADO
TRANSLATED BY ROBERT BLY

Close your eyes and notice the quality of your breath. Does it feel even, hurried, tense, deep, or sparse? Bringing attention to your breath is a meditation practice in itself, one that you can do each morning, each evening, or throughout the day to center yourself. Follow your breath as it moves up and down your front torso, in front of your spine, and along your *sushumna* (the central energy channel that flows from the base to the crown *chakra. Chakras* are the flowerlike energy centers in the body that was first written about in ancient Hindu texts). Say prayers or intentions if you like, quietly out loud to yourself, and let go of any worry. Take time to speak your heart's truth and longing. As thoughts come, let them pass like clouds; don't cling to anything about yourself or the daily distractions and details of your life. This is a time for your mind to rest and your heart to fill with gratitude for your existence. Be patient with yourself; meditation can be challenging in the beginning. With time, you can build the quality and duration of your practice. For now, allow the blossoms of your heart to unfold with wonder.

[BELOW, TOP: MEDITATION CAN BE SIMPLY THOUGHT OF AS A TIME YOU GIVE TO YOURSELF TO BE WITH YOUR BREATH AND ENJOY SOME SILENCE AND QUIETUDE.]

[BELOW, BOTTOM: SETTING INTENTIONS OR PRAYERS CAN HELP DEEPEN MEDITATION EXPERIENCE.]

[SHOWN HERE IS A MIXED-MEDIA COLLAGE WITH PRINTED IMAGES, DOILIES, PAINT, GEL PENS, AND ACRYLICS.]

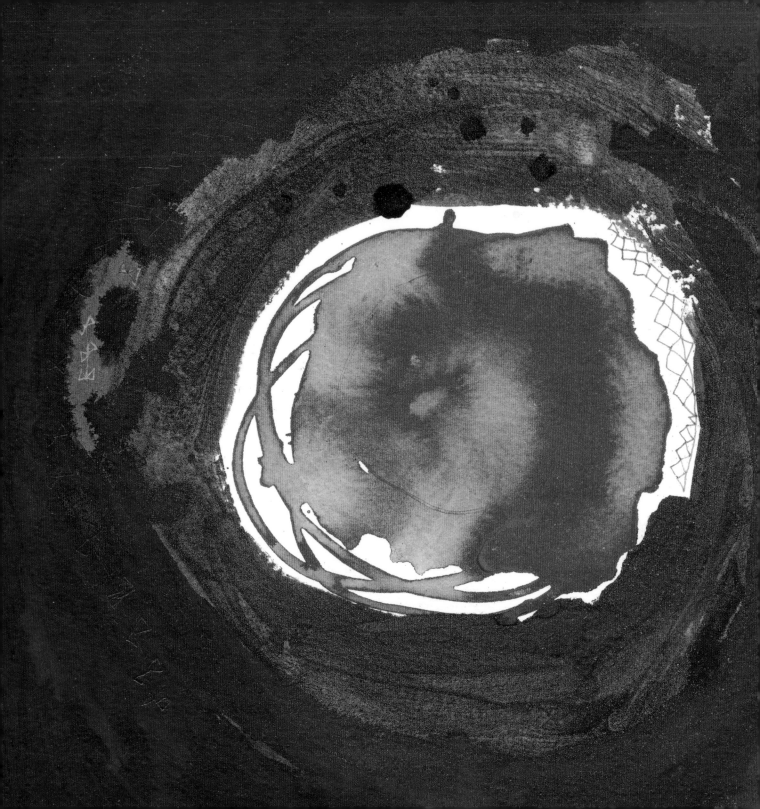

 **EXERCISE** # Consider

Write about the following below.

» How do you feel about your internal state? What is it calling out or longing for? What do you feel will help calm and ease you emotionally?

_____

_____

_____

_____

_____

» How do you feel such Eastern practices as yoga and *pranayama* will benefit your art making? Is there any concern that centering yourself will compromise the duality that compels you to make work? For instance, do you feel that clinging to unbalanced emotional states may help fuel your expression? Explore this; you may uncover something juicy.

_____

_____

_____

_____

_____

 **EXERCISE** # Create

» Set aside a space in your home to contemplate, meditate, and/or practice yoga. Make this space a respite where you can sit and be quiet, stretch, write, space out: whatever you need to rejuvenate your spirit.

 **EXERCISE** # Release and Intend

» An emotional release painting can be done completely on instinct. Play with bold colors, experiment, doodle without thinking or censuring your marks, and allow whatever comes through you to just come without judgment. Flick, scratch, tear, burn, or even finger paint. Make it a tangible experience with no rules. Give yourself permission to play and get dirty.

» Make an intentional art piece that calls to bring more balance and nourishment into your life. Create a collage by cutting out words and letters from a book or magazine and paint around it in colors that feel soothing. Use old papers or writings that have significant meaning to you. Collect images and find decorative papers to paste down using glue. Draw around the words in pen or a fine-tip marker. Place this simple piece on your altar or meditation space if you have one. Perhaps you would like to embellish it with fine glitter to give it sparkle, or seal it with a liquid varnish to preserve it.

TRY THIS!

» If you have not tried a yoga class before, now is a perfect time to see if it's for you. I suggest a gentle or level 1 class at first. Go to a studio that has been recommended by friends.

» If you already are familiar with yoga classes, begin a simple practice each morning for a week, even if it's just a few stretches for fifteen minutes. After the week is done, make note about whether it had any effect on you. Notice the way you feel after practicing. Write down those feelings in a journal. Try making some art after yoga as well. Did you notice anything different?

» Try another physical practice if yoga does not call you. Tai chi and qigong are some other options from the East. I personally find joy in a dance or movement class that I try to attend several times a week. This really helps me get out of my head and into my body, along with letting me release physical or emotional tension. Just try anything that will connect you to your breath and your center while practicing movement.

» Before working on your next art piece, take time to close your eyes and meditate on what you would like this piece to look and feel like. Perhaps you already do this in some fashion anyway. So, take some time and follow your breath in and out of your body, such as in *deergha swasam* or three-part breath (see page 88). After this process feels complete, begin to immediately create.

TIP OF THE TRADE

Before a big event or taking a risk, take some time to center yourself and set some intentions. Write them down if you would like. This can be done anytime you feel nervous to present, network, or even put yourself "out there" with your art. People respond well to a relaxed and clear person, and this may help you communicate more clearly and effectively.

Seek out shows on both local and national levels. Look for places recommended by other artists and research online to find places that exhibit similar work as yours. Even approaching a favorite local café is a great way to start. Salons, restaurants, health food stores, record stores, boutiques, and other places of business may be open to exhibiting artwork as well. Showing your work in more places brings it more attention and more opportunity, which in turn can encourage you to create more.

Sometimes people need to see something several times before they buy it; they need to form a relationship with the piece before they feel comfortable enough to purchase it. With that in mind, do not hesitate to share your work on the Web and with family and friends as well as in galleries. For example, go ahead and create a Facebook fan page for your art or business. As long as you have a decent set of photographs, it takes almost no time at all. The encouragement you receive will be a great motivator and may also lead to some sales.

[OPPOSITE: PRACTICING YOGA WITH A FRIEND OR IN A CLASS HELPS TO KEEP YOU MOTIVATED.

[ABOVE: A COLLAGE ON GIVING YOURSELF A MOMENT TO BECOME CENTERED]

"Do your practice and all is coming." —SRI K. PATTABHI JOIS

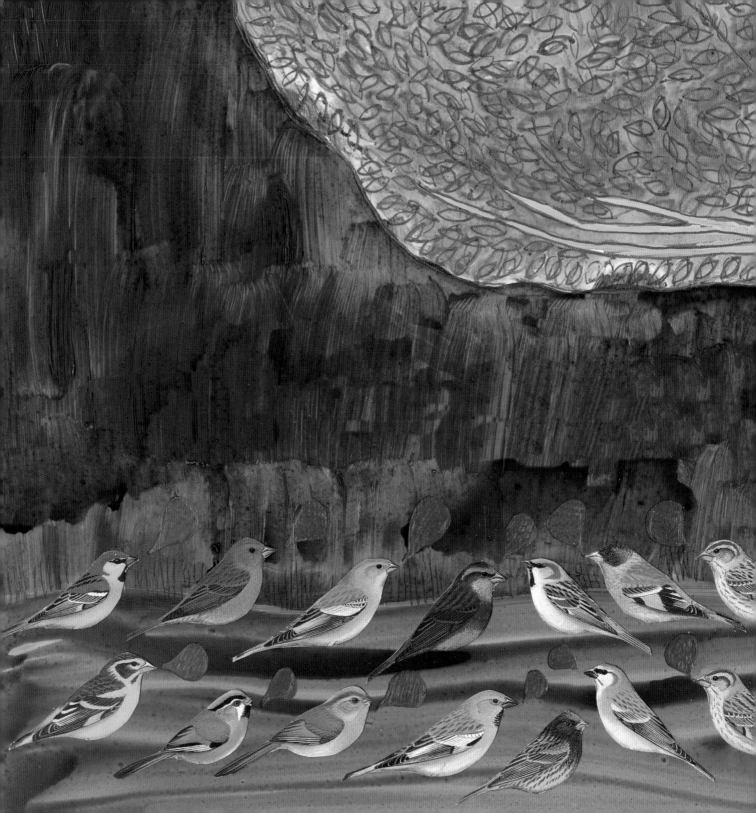

CHAPTER 7

Roots & Branches

So, what does it take not only to survive but also to thrive as an artist? Some may say luck or raw talent. But I happen to believe that a good part of success is based on action. It is my personal thought that energy is the building block of life, and when you put energy into the world through creative work and action, the universe must respond. Positive action brings positive response.

There is certainly some fear involved: fear of rejection, fear of being broke, and fear of failure. But getting wrapped up in fear only restricts your work and prevents you from taking action. Only by working with consistency and resolve do our lives begin to change.

[LEARNING TO FULLY LISTEN HELPS US UNDERSTAND THE SITUATIONS AROUND US.]

"Do you want to know who you are? Don't ask. Act! Action will delineate and define you."

—THOMAS JEFFERSON

[FLOAT SMOOTHLY INTO THE DIRECTION OF YOUR DREAMS.]

For me, taking action means creating and sharing my work on a regular basis. And it goes beyond sitting in the studio and working. Attending that art opening or gathering to socialize and network can be taking action.

One breakthrough for me that involved taking action was attending the New York International Gift Fair. A lot of the press I initially received came from that show and got my career off to a solid start. I also made licensing deals with several companies to use my art on their products, for either royalties or a flat fee.

Before I attended the show, however, I went to just check it out. I studied booth displays, the inner workings of the fair, and how it all came together. After I traveled back home, I prepared my application. I wanted to be accepted into one of the juried sections for artists, designers, or crafters.

Once I was accepted, I set some goals for myself. I wanted to receive a certain number of new wholesale accounts, along with making more contacts with press and possible licensing deals. I spoke these goals out loud to my partner before the show began.

When the show finally came, I was overwhelmed with joy when I had a line for buyers waiting to place orders just as my booth was opening. This was several years ago, and I know things may have changed since then at wholesale shows. Still, that experience was instrumental for me at the start of my career. I did, in fact, not only meet my goals, but I also surpassed them.

Please know that attending a wholesale trade show can be a huge undertaking. Lately, I mostly sell retail out of my studio storefront, along with on my website. Store buyers and licensors tend to find me solely through my website now. I may exhibit at trade shows again someday, but the direction of my career has taken me on a different course as of late.

"Follow effective action with quiet reflection. From the quiet reflection will come even more effective action." —PETER DRUCKER

Listening can be intrinsically linked to later action. It helps us become aware of what is happening now and where we should move next. Through listening and observing, our senses become sharper and our intuition can speak to us.

As we learn to become still and heighten our awareness with the help of such practices as yoga and meditation, our intuition steps in, tells us where to move next, and helps us through our creative work. It allows us to act on instinct, which gives us room to play. As children we thrive on our instinctual nature, moving from this to that. You can easily see this when you observe children making art. I believe that in every adult there is a child who wants to come out and play, and how wonderful it is to access that when we get to work.

Instinct can also help us in our art careers. For instance, I may hear a call to enter a group show held at a local museum or gallery, and I just get a "gut feeling" I should submit my work. One instance I can recall was when I was living in Miami and was part of an artist residency in the Design District. A local museum put out a call for the "Best of Florida" show and I immediately knew which painting I should submit. I was not a well-known artist at this time and knew it could be a long shot to be accepted, yet I just had a feeling that this painting, a

mixed-media piece with dozens of varying glass balls and beads, with a digital photo of a white peacock covered in resin, would be accepted. It did, in fact, and it was a lovely experience and an exhibit I could add to my résumé. After press got out about the show, another gallery contacted me soon after that. This chain reaction of creative abundance was set forth all because I heard a little voice that said, "Try this."

Our heart's deepest desires, our longings, that buzzing feeling that wants to come forth and shine bright for the world, those are things to trust. As we listen more and more to ourselves, feelings like pain, sadness, and regret may bubble up along with the good feelings. This is all part of the process. We need to allow those emotions to come, hold them like a baby, care for them without judgment, and allow them to pass through and out of our beings. Tending to your inner garden sometimes means pulling out weeds and tossing them in the compost heap.

The deep spring of the soul is vast and mysterious; breathe into it with care, patience, and reverence so that the spring can well up and fill your being even more. From that spring, beautiful things around it begin to grow, starting from the inside and manifesting out. This is how transformation in your life can take place. You are a bright, beautiful being that has come to this world to share such unique gifts. You are meant to shine.

My Longshot Ideas:

"Intuition is a spiritual faculty and does not explain, but simply points the way."

—FLORENCE SCOVEL SHINN

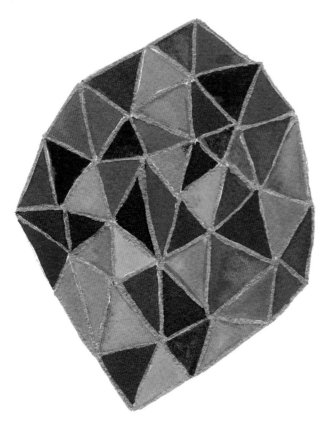

[WE EACH HAVE SUCH MULTIFACETED AND UNIQUE QUALITIES OR SHADES OF BEING.]

"The creative is the place where no one else has ever been. You have to leave the city of your comfort and go into the wilderness of your intuition." —ALAN ALDA

It's also important to understand the small but vast difference between action and reaction. Positive action taken from events and circumstances in our lives creates change and forward movement. Reaction comes from a place of fear, or a need to control the situation. Reacting to life's challenges in a place that feels emotionally ungrounded or unsettling can diminish our creative vitality and ability to truly move forward. Reacting to others' success through mental comparison is not helpful, either; neither is feeling diminished by setbacks or rejections. Understand that your

life is unfolding just as it should. Trust has a wonderful way of birthing new things in life and putting us into the natural rhythm of existence.

So, take positive action from the things that occur in your life and celebrate the success of others. I know that when I celebrate others' success, it has a contagious energy to it, and my efforts to reach out are returned. Tips are shared, encouragement is given, and achievement can sometimes be a communal process. I have several artist friends whom I know I can call on to help me out if I am having trouble with something, or need advice—and they can do the same with me. That feeling of camaraderie builds an authentic network of friends. Plus, as you find joy in others' happiness or success, your own personal joy increases, maybe because we are all so interconnected, sometimes more than we realize.

bliss / **blis**

noun / blis

: total happiness : < she fell softly to sleep in complete *bliss* > :

: heaven, infinite delight < the state of sheer *bliss* is possible in this life > :

: origin : first known use: before the 12th century < Middle English *blisse*; similar to Old English *blithe* > :

—or—

blissed-out

adj blist-'aut

: to fully experience bliss or total ecstasy :

My Deepest Desires:

My Deepest Desires:

"If you want others to be happy, practice compassion. If you want to be happy, practice compassion."

—DALAI LLAMA

"What should young people do with their lives today? Many things, obviously. But the most daring thing is to create stable communities in which the terrible disease of loneliness can be cured." —KURT VONNEGUT JR.

Another important branch in your creative tree of life is a supportive community. A network of colleagues who do what you do is a wonderful resource to have; they can be instrumental and helpful in many ways not thought possible. Here in the River Arts District in Asheville, North Carolina, where I live, we have more than 100 working artists sharing experiences in a small but beautiful tourist town. It can be very comforting to know you are part of something and not alone in your process or work as an artist. A lot of little tidbits and helpful information are passed along, from which space to exhibit at to which tourist trolley car actually buys art, to which month to expect sales to increase, and so forth.

If you live in a more isolated area, you can connect to an online creative community that stretches around the world. I cannot emphasize enough the benefit of this. The online world has helped create my livelihood—and I have made some lovely friends because of it as well. I have planned numerous group shows with artists I have met online, and sometimes have asked to create a guest blog on a friend's popular blog, which helps draw traffic to my website. Online art friends have been kind enough to share what really worked for them, as well as passed my name on to a press contact or licensing company and given me a recommendation. None of this is very time-consuming, either, since most of it is done through email. Plus, it's totally fun to connect with my Bay Area or New York peers with a simple tweet or Facebook comment. It keeps us all feeling connected, and perhaps inspired and motivated.

Friendships made in the spirit of creativity seem to have a special bond that runs deep in mutual respect and support. One of the first friends I made online was Ashley Alexander (creator of I'm Smitten) from Chicago. We did a painting and print trade and shared our experiences with certain galleries/boutiques that we both sold to. She contributed to a children's book I did years ago as well. I also got to interview her for an indie art magazine, which was loads of fun. I finally met her in person when we both exhibited at the Renegade Craft Fair. It was sweet to see the painting I had first sent her some six years ago.

[A COMMUNITY TREE COLLAGE]

> "When it is obvious that the goals cannot be reached, don't adjust the goals, adjust the action steps."
> —CONFUCIUS

[HERE I AM ADDING FINER DETAILS TO THIS PAINTING USING GEL PENS.]

 **EXERCISE** # Contemplate

Write about the following in your sketchbook:

» When you close your eyes and center yourself, what does your intuition tell you about your passions and goals? What steps do you need to take to direct them on a more fulfilling path? Write about this in your journal. Do not edit or censure yourself. Let your writing hand become a channel for your higher self, and let the words move through you from a greater source.

_____
_____
_____
_____
_____
_____
_____
_____
_____
_____

 **EXERCISE** # Collaborate

» Make a collaborative piece with an art friend. This can be a really fulfilling process along with a way to push your boundaries and merge your creative skills and instincts with someone else's. Collaboration can take many forms—from a painting or sculpture, to a photo series, handmade book, journal share, performance piece, or anything! Make sure both of you take time to discuss the project—what you want to get out of it, your vision, and so on. In other words, "get on the same page" but allow each person to stay true to his or her authenticity. If conflict arises due to creative differences, take time to talk about it and create agreements so that everyone involved can feel comfortable. It may be helpful for each of you to do an art piece on your own initially and then discuss ways you can both see your artistic temperaments coming together.

 # EXERCISE Intuit

» Make an intuitive drawing (something I absolutely adore doing)! Take a piece of paper and a colored pen. Put on some mellow tunes if you'd like, and close your eyes. Begin to draw and move your hand around, going completely on instinct. Do this for a little bit and then open your eyes. Color in the shapes with paint, gel pens, watercolor pencils, or India ink. Next, do the same sort of drawing but with your eyes open. Do not think about what you are doing—just move your hand around instinctively. Make creative decisions here and there, but try to breathe into your heart and let this be a meditative experience. Push the paint around with your fingers, doodle on the edges, write words of inspiration and intention; just let it move out from and through you.

[AFTER YOU HAVE DRAWN AN INTUITIVE DRAWING
BY CLOSING YOUR EYES, YOU CAN FILL IN THE SHAPES
WITH COLORS AND DETAILS.]

TRY THIS!

» If you do not already have a community you feel tapped into, begin to explore some possibilities. Look for the nearest art studios, centers, cafés—anyplace where community and creativity are a focus. See what you find there; see if the atmosphere calls to you. Look for workshops that spark your interest. Take some steps to reach out and trust the process of trying something new. If you are already tapped into a community, take more steps to reach out.

» Create an art and craft night with some friends. Get some wine, tea, and treats and have everyone bring his or her own materials. You can create stations with yarn, papers, paints, beads, oil pastels, and more. Designate a time to meet every month and rotate hosting duties. I absolutely love doing this! A lot of lively talk can be had over art and craft materials.

» Organize a group show in your area with some of your favorite artists or friends. Approach each artist with your idea and then local galleries, shops, or cafés. Have a few meetings with each participant to talk about all the details of the show. Create a press release in enough time before the show to send to local papers. You can also start out simple and just have a little group show in your own home! Throw an opening-night party and celebrate the work you all have done.

TIP OF THE TRADE

To further tap into an artist community locally as well as online, have your website, blog, and/or Facebook fan or group page in place. If you need to start simply, create a blog with your work; just be sure to have good photographs or scans. Look at various blogging sites and compare each for your needs: TypePad, Blogspot, Tumblr, and WordPress are some popular ones. Create a theme and then decide what type of content you would like to consistently share. Research books or browse the Internet for the best approach to starting your blog. Get ideas from other resources, but be sure to make your blog unique. Let it be true to you and your creative spirit. You will want to take photos often, so a digital camera is a valuable tool to have.

You can use your Facebook page as your way to blog, or to get your feet wet with sharing work. Ask to trade links with fellow artists who blog and feel free to write about artists' work that inspires you.

Etsy, the online arts and crafts site, is also a great way to showcase and sell your work if you are not ready to create a website. Even if you already have a website, having an Etsy page can complement it.

To further connect to artists online, begin to read blogs, make comments, and "friend" sites you like. Let this be a natural process, however—don't force it. Little by little things happen. Make sure your work is your focus. You can get sucked into the online world quickly, and the next thing you know several hours have passed.

Seek advice from those you can relate to. Observe what feels right to you and follow that. I have found that being connected regionally is also helpful; I love my Southeast region of artists, from Raleigh to Atlanta to Athens. If you are already connected online, deepen your connections through simple action-based steps. Perhaps you would like to begin attending and applying to indie craft fairs or art fairs, which happen all over the United States. Do your research. Some of those can be quite lucrative, while others are just plain exhausting with very little payoff. Getting a firsthand recommendation is always best. Know your limits and what is going to serve you in the end.

"Our deepest fears are like dragons guarding our deepest treasure."

—RAINER MARIA RILKE

"Beware what you set your heart upon,
for it surely shall be yours."

—RALPH WALDO EMERSON

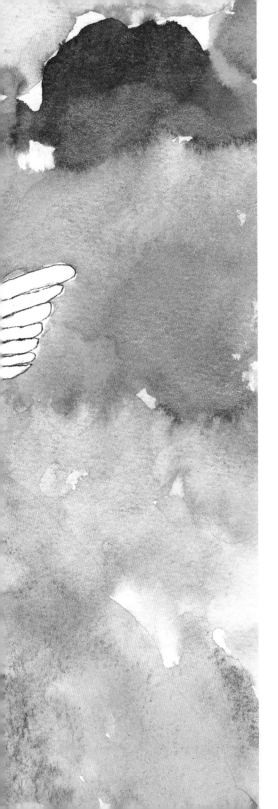

CHAPTER 8

Tools to Manifest

Think of the human heart as a flower. What does a flower need to bloom? It needs nourishment from the elements of water and light, along with a proper foundation. Slowly, with care and attention, a bud grows, and then the petals begin to open. During that process of blossoming, a flower emits a distinctive fragrance, one that we get to take pleasure in. Bees then begin to come, buzzing, searching, and collecting the nectar that they are so attracted to. And so the cycle of life continues, with the natural laws of attraction in place. The sunflower is attracted to the sun, the bees and hummingbirds to nectar, and human beings to all the pleasures we take in with our senses.

[THINGS IN LIFE CAN SOMETIMES REFLECT BACK
TO US LIKE A MIRROR.]

So, how does nature or the universe respond to that which you set your heart and mind upon? Throughout time, many writers and philosophers have shared that whatever you truly desire is yours to attain; that the universe will provide. This has been true for me in my little art world. Not all of it goes according to plan, of course, and there are many unexpected twists and turns that can take place, for that is the nature of life. But overall, it is uncanny how much has manifested in my life just as I wanted it. I find it especially clear in my art career. To share an example, a year ago I asked for a ground floor studio space that got a lot of foot traffic and wasn't going to rob me blind financially. I saw the space clear in my mind and within nine months I got a call out of the blue from the building owner who remembered me once inquiring about space. She had a rare opening at a very coveted space and happened to like my work, so she was contacting me as a long shot. I was not even residing in Asheville at the time, but in a place where I was making decisions about my next steps in life, and asking the universe for guidance. So this studio space I am in now is a dream come true. It's so close to what I had envisioned.

But to get to this place, first you must know your heart, understand its desires, and give it attention and care, just like a flower, so it may bloom. Practice thinking positive thoughts and vibrate energetically in states of peace and acceptance. Imagine what it would feel like if those things you desire were already real, which is a foundational rule of the laws of attraction. Trust that all is being provided to you, and perhaps most importantly, believe in yourself and your talents. Confidence goes a long way in this world, as do authenticity and kindness. Kindness is contagious, as is happiness. So seek out those who uplift and support your dreams; it will be that much easier to vibrate from a place of love and kindness.

In addition, like attracts like—the more we give, the more we receive just what we have given. There are challenges in between, but they can sometimes serve as our greatest teachers. So be free from judgment of yourself and others. See that nothing you have done is a mistake, just a teaching for you to further you along your path. See the universe and your time on Earth as a time to love and serve all. Every day is a gift, and we never know when it will be our time to go.

Life can be incredibly hard and disappointing at times. But with steady practice, as the blossoms of your heart begin to open with love, you will have a magnificent garden that is uniquely yours and you can always find comfort in. In fact, you have that garden now. It's just lifting the veils of doubt and insecurity to accept that the garden is yours for your keeping and cultivation.

"There are only two ways to live your life. One is as though nothing is a miracle. The other is as if everything is." —ALBERT EINSTEIN

"Love is what we are born with. Fear is what we learn. The spiritual journey is the unlearning of fear and prejudices and the acceptance of love back in our hearts. Love is the essential reality and our purpose on earth. To be consciously aware of it, to experience love in ourselves and others, is the meaning of life. Meaning does not lie in things. Meaning lies in us." —MARIANNE WILLIAMSON

One big break that I received in the beginning of my career was to have my art featured in several well-known magazines. How this happened was incredibly simple. I sent one of my handmade bird sculptures addressed as a gift to the editor of the section for which I was submitting my work, wrapped in a white box with ribbon, along with a straightforward handwritten note, a business card, and an "About the Artist" card. I think two out of three of my favorite magazines that I contacted gave me press.

I believe this is part of the laws of attraction—to give out of the sheer joy of giving, and by dropping expectations of what should happen. I had no idea what to expect; I was just delighted that I was taking action. So when I received a positive response, I was, of course, very grateful.

I also believe that gratitude is an essential practice to manifesting your dreams. Starting out right where you are and noticing what you are grateful for makes everything feel fresh and new. If I'm feeling down or dumpy about something, I try to shift to thinking about things I am grateful for. It really can turn a crummy day into a bright experience.

There are so many things to feel grateful for, both small and big. When I begin to think about the thousands and thousands of people who are suffering in this world, who are dying of hunger and living in appalling conditions, I sometimes can't believe my good fortune and grace. When we take our thinking from the small self to the bigger self for the benefit of all humanity, shifts in our being begin to happen, and we can start to take action to help others. That feeling of self-pity can turn into benevolence; anger can turn into action, and sadness into compassion for others' suffering. Just showing kindness or helping out a stranger can send rippling effects into the universe.

> *"Your mind is a tool you can choose to use any way you wish."* —LOUISE HAY

[A COLLAGE EXHIBITING THE CONCEPT OF "LIKE ATTRACTS LIKE"]

Gratitude, when paired with acceptance, may also help you to forgive others. It can help make sense of the past and allow you to let go of it, accepting that things happened as they did. It can also shift your perception about what is unique and beautiful in your life, and how the things in our lives help form who we are today. When we forgive others, we become liberated and free from the experience that hurt us. The more attachment, expectation, and control we place on others, the more suffering we experience. People will never act exactly how we want them to, and things don't always go as planned, but if we learn to live in states of acceptance, with, of course, respect for our own needs, we can feel so much more peace in our lives. Forgiveness is a constant practice, a way of being, not just a onetime act. A wonderful benefit of practicing forgiveness is that it brings happiness.

What would it be like to live a life of total gratitude? If everything you looked upon—your house, your loved ones, your food, and your clothes, no matter what the shape, size, color, or quality—seemed like an incredible gift? Now see that life transforming into something even greater. How would that feel? From this place you can create a platform for a greater tomorrow. This is because you begin to accept and not fight where you are, and thus feel moved to make changes for the better. When I am feeling grateful for things in my life, I also seem to receive more things to feel grateful for.

I am grateful for:

[WHAT THINGS OF GRACE IN YOUR LIFE CAN YOU BEGIN TO
FEEL THANKFUL FOR?]

*"If you want to turn your life around, try thankfulness.
It will change your life mightily."* —GERALD GOOD

[THIS PAINTING SHOWS MY THANKS FOR SOMEONE SPECIAL IN MY LIFE.]

"Cherish your visions and your dreams as they are the children of your soul, the blueprints of your ultimate achievements."

—NAPOLEON HILL

EXERCISE Ruminate

Write about the following:

» How can you begin to become what your heart desires, starting right now? If your heart is longing for companionship, try giving true companionship to yourself or the people you are with from moment to moment. In other words, be totally present for yourself and others. Don't be hard on yourself with negative thoughts or push away others when they reach out.

_____

_____

_____

_____

_____

_____

» What are some things, or people, that you are grateful for? Make a list. Make it as complete as possible.

_____

_____

_____

_____

_____

_____

» What are some intentions you wish to set forth in your life, starting today? Setting intentions are ways to call forth what you want to manifest in your life. Write statements starting with "I am," "I have," and "It is." Imagine that it is your reality now.

_____

_____

_____

_____

_____

_____

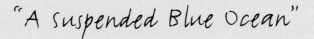
"A suspended Blue Ocean"

The sky
Is a suspended blue ocean.
The stars are the fish
That swim.

The planets are the white whales
I sometimes hitch a ride on,

And the sun and all light
Have forever fused themselves

Into my heart and upon
My skin.

There is only one rule
On this Wild Playground,

For every sign Hafiz has ever seen
Reads the same.

They all say,

"Have fun, my dear; my dear, have fun,
In the Beloved's Divine
Game,

O, in the Beloved's
Wonderful Game."

—HAFIZ

 # Create and Manifest

» Take your list of intentional "I am" statements and illustrate these things in your journal. This is a loose sketch exercise—it's quite all right if they look childlike! Draw details. For example, if you have written "I am living with my life partner in a beautiful home that has a lovely garden of flowers and vegetables," draw the kinds of flowers and vegetables you'd have. What does your home look like on the outside? The inside? Draw your life partner, your family.

"Abundance is not something we acquire. It is something we tune into ...Within you is the divine capacity to manifest and attract all that you need or desire."

—DR. WAYNE DYER

[MY HEART COLLAGE]

Go Further

Make a collage of your inside world. Bring in colors, animals, lines, shapes, objects, places, or anything else that expresses your inner self. Paint paper and cut out things that give detail to your collage. If needed, make another collage of the inside world you would like to experience. One thing to think about is that our inside world and outside world can be in harmony, so bring in things that represent your desires in both realms.

[EVERYTHING BEGINS TO FEEL CONNECTED WHEN I SLOW DOWN TO THE RHYTHM OF NATURE.]

TRY THIS!

» Practice random acts of kindness to others. Reach out when someone seems in need. Offer some warm words or assurance. Phone someone you've been meaning to call and tell this person how much you love him or her.

People I Love:

» Act as if the success you seek is already yours, as if you could not fail. If you knew there was no risk and if you could only succeed, what steps would you be taking in your life right now? This is an exercise to begin changing your thought process and thus believing and radiating that success out into the world. Know that nothing can hold you back from attaining your heart's deepest dreams.

» Set some intentions for yourself daily. Sometimes I speak out loud a goal of a dollar amount I would like to sell out of my gallery space for that day or week. It's surprising how close the sales can end up being to my spoken goal.

TIP OF THE TRADE

I want the last tip in this book to be less something "to do" and more something "to be." If we can begin to change the way we see things in our lives, those things in our lives begin to change. So let go of where you think you should be and begin to see the gift of the present moment: to love and accept what is and where you are right now. In the present moment is the only place where we are breathing; where we are truly living: it's when we begin to grow and shift the focus of our lives from "trying" to "allowing, being, and receiving," from "surviving" to "thriving," thus cultivating more success and joy. Wherever you are right now is exactly where you need to be.

You can also never go wrong with being yourself. By being and also believing in yourself you can continue on the path of your dreams and tend to your highest purpose. You have so many gifts to share, and the world needs your light to shine out, so shine bright, dear star. You are truly beautiful.

"The greatest revolution in our generation is that of human beings, who by changing the inner attitudes of their minds can change the outer aspects of their lives."

—WILLIAM JAMES

I am beautiful.

About the Author

Alena Hennessy is an artist recognized in the online world of art and craft. Her work has been published in *Dwell*, *Readymade*, *Redbook*, *Natural Health*, the *Washington Post*, *ME Home Companion*, *Victoria*, and numerous design blogs. Her paintings and wares can be found in boutiques and galleries in the United States and abroad.

Alena is also a practitioner in the healing arts and teaches e-courses and workshops in the United States on transformation and manifestation through the creative process. She calls the beautiful mountains in Asheville, North Carolina, her home, where you can also find her studio and showroom.

Visit Alena online at www.alenahennessy.com.

© STEVE MANN

Acknowledgments

Many hands help make work a little lighter ...

Sincere thanks to Daisy Marquis, Michael Birnberg, Nicole McConville, Brooke Sullivan, Bloom Post, Alexander J. Caruso, Elizabeth MacCrellish, Mary Aarons, Steve Mann, and Andrew Bowers.

I would also like to thank my steady and grounded editor, Mary Ann Hall, for understanding and believing in my vision.

Pattiy Torno, my friend and studio mate—thank you for holding down the fort during many a late night that crossed over into day.

Doah Chabot and Ruslan Tumash, my collaborators for *Breathing Deep*: Doah, thank you for your grace and talent, and for being such a beautiful yogini. Ruslan, you always seem to capture the unique brilliance of light in your photos. Thank you for your time and skill.

Colette Johnson, my assistant extraordinaire, your exceptional beauty runs as deeply inside as it is shown on the outside.

Finally, Jane Ellen Hennessy, my goddess of a mother and best friend: Your belief and support in what I do has helped form who I am today. This book is dedicated to you. I love you.

Dream big. Dream bold. Love the
life you live.

✳